PRAISE FOR SMA

"Brad Lewis brings his many years of small group leadership, his commitment to biblical teaching, and his passion for authentic relationships to an impressive intersection in *Small Group University*. Without a doubt, this is a valuable and effective resource to equip Christian leaders of all ages. Today more than ever, our world needs a demonstration of excellence, authenticity, and doctrinal soundness. This book deserves a spot on your bookshelf. Let's get out there and reach more people!"

–Rob Ketterling
Lead Pastor, River Valley Church, Minneapolis MN
Author of *Change Before You Have To*

"*Small Group University* is a unique and timely manifesto on the ancient- future dynamic of what makes for Book of Acts change agents for this hour. Brad does an exceptional job of both inspiring and giving us tools to catalyze new breed constructors of cultural change through discipleship and small groups. To Brad these concepts are not just theories but a reflection of life principles from the epic journey that he has walked. I have seen both his life and fruit up close and I've come away inspired and I am sure that you will too as you read and apply these truths."

–Sean Smith
Author of *I Am Your Sign & Prophetic Evangelism*
(www.seansmithministries.com) @RevSeanSmith

"Through his book, *Small Group University, Relevant Training For The Emerging Leader*, Brad Lewis addresses a veritable need in Chi Alpha and all campus ministry: the structure and development of effective small group ministry. Brad's pragmatic and adroit approach to the ministry of small groups will lend excellent structure and priorities for all those in campus ministry. His three decades of fruitful ministry to university students has ripened his writing with wisdom and practical insight. This resource will serve campus ministers as well as student leaders in the fulfillment of their mission on campus to raise up men and women of God."

—E. Scott Martin

National Director, Chi Alpha Campus Ministries

"This book is summarizing a culture of small groups that has been spreading across the U.S. over the last 10 years. It's not about methods as much as capturing God's heart for the individual, positioning every leader to be a person of influence in their generation. It's time for more pastors and directors to empower and equip their leaders to do the work of the mission. *Small Group University* will help us do it!"

—Drew Meyer

District Director, Iowa Chi Alpha Campus Ministries

"I have a confession, I have never been to a small group led by Brad Lewis... But I have been around small groups, larger groups, and leaders that are part of Brad's ministry. I can honestly say that this is one of the most dynamic, healthy, growing communities that I have been around. At the heart of this health is their commitment to small groups. *Small Group University* communicates heart, value, and strategy behind the development of healthy small groups, and their impact on their community. As a former small group pastor, I highly recommend this book to pastors, small group leaders or anyone who aspires to lead a group in the future. *Small Group University* is not only easy to understand, it will inspire you, give you firm biblical grounding, and a sound strategy for building healthy groups."

—Paul Hurckman

Executive Director, Venture Expeditions

"Pastor Brad Lewis personifies Spirit-led ministry that touches hearts time and again. As he has trained others in the secrets of caring small group ministry, thousands have been transformed by the power of Christ. His book comes from years of fruitful ministry and is an insightful, practical guide for anyone desiring a flourishing group ministry. Put this on your 'must read' list!"

−Dr. Bob Ona
Lead Pastor, First Assembly, Fargo ND

"Aided by decades of ministry experience, Brad Lewis has effectively produced a model for ministry that creates community, empowers individuals and reproduces leaders. *Small Group University* is not only a manual for your small group leaders, it's also a recipe for revival in your mission field. If you have found yourself or your church struggling to live empowered and outward-reaching, this book will teach you how to make disciples in a practical and relational way. We were made for this."

−Josh Skjoldal
Young Adults Pastor, Evangel Assembly, Bismarck ND

"Brad Lewis is an inspiration! I have friends that have been raised up under his leadership and sent out who are now influencing hundreds of young adults all over the country. His insight on how to build a successful small group system will help any leader at any level of an organization or church. Brad focuses on the heart Jesus had for relationships while He was on the earth and how we can live that out in our own lives today. I would recommend this book not only for young adults, but for the seasoned ministry leaders who have a heart for building relationships and community in their cities, neighborhoods, and schools."

−Kirk Graham
20+ Pastor, River Valley Church, Minneapolis MN

"In *Small Group University*, Brad Lewis meets a critical need in an inspiring way. During years of evangelistic ministry on the road, I have rarely seen such effective training in motion for healthy faith community. I have observed the fruit from this teach firsthand…

In fact...NOBODY does it better! This book will be my 'go-to' recommendation for small group leader training."

—Mark Zweifel
Director, Impact Alaska, Inc.
Lead Pastor, First Assembly, Fairbanks AK

"Some people 'write about discipleship' and some people 'breath discipleship', Brad Lewis does both. In his new book, *Small Group University*, Brad addresses vital topics like how to build a group, conduct a one-on-one, pray for people, and maintain a high moral standard as a leader. In the end, Brad reminds us that the key to biblical discipleship is deep relationship. *Small Group University* will bless you and your ministry regardless of the age demographic you serve."

—Curtis Cole
Administrative Director, Chi Alpha Campus Ministries

FOREWORD BY DR. JAMES BRADFORD

SMALL GROUP
UNIVERSITY

RELEVANT TRAINING FOR THE EMERGING LEADER

REV. BRAD LEWIS

ISBN: 9780-9906187-2-0

*This book is dedicated to my beautiful wife, Kay,
and my two children, Daniel and Rachel. Thank you
for your endless love, encouragement, and support! I love you!*

CONTENTS

ACKNOWLEDGEMENTS

To my wife, Kay—You are my babe. I love you, honey. Thank you for believing in me and for being my biggest fan. I can't even describe how awesome it has been to serve God with you, to raise a family with you, and to do ministry with you.

To my son, Daniel—I love being your dad. You are the best hunting partner I could ask for. I am so proud of you as I watch the call of God develop on your life. I love you.

To my daughter, Rachel—I love being your dad. You bring so much joy to my life. I love your tender heart and sensitive spirit. You are becoming a beautiful woman of God.

To my parents—Dad, I am so happy that you are still here to read this. I can't thank you and mom enough for shaping a heart of love in me.

To my current staff and their spouses—Nate and Whitney, Dave and Alissa, Dave and Sara, Steve and Erin, and Stephen—Thank you for all the help writing this book, but mostly for being my best friends. I love you.

To Tony and Kayla—Thank you for our deep relationship, the many years of ministry together, and for bouncing so many of these ideas around years ago. Tony, thank you for being a best friend. I am so proud of you and love you.

To Pastor Bob and Sharon—Thank you for the years of believing in me and encouraging me. You have made my dream possible.

To my cousins—Joey and Tony—Thank you for giving your love and time to a spiritually hungry young man.

1 Thessalonians 2:7-8

"But we proved to be gentle among you, as a nursing mother tenderly cares for her own children. Having so fond an affection for you, we were well-pleased to impart to you not only the gospel of God but also our own lives, because you had become very dear to us."

Ephesians 4:29

"Let no unwholesome word proceed from your mouth, but only such a word as is good for edification according to the need of the moment, so that it will give grace to those who hear."

FOREWORD

It was not until my freshman year in college that I first heard the word 'disciple' used as a verb. It was a groundbreaking moment in my budding perception of what ministry leadership could be.

As a university student I was familiar with 'lecturer' and 'class.' One of my favorite teachers was a fluid mechanics professor in the Aerospace Department at the University of Minnesota. Although I did not know him personally, I learned and would often be inspired as I sat under his teaching. But when that same fluid mechanics professor invited me to become his graduate research assistant, my educational experience fundamentally changed. It shifted from a 'classroom' experience to a 'discipleship' experience. The difference? Relationship and personal mentoring.

My rich Pentecostal heritage, dating back to early childhood, left me with a high view of personal encounters with the Holy Spirit and Jesus' mission in the world. However, to 'disciple' someone into becoming a mature follower of Jesus was a revolutionary concept. It was a ministry philosophy that would require what I later experienced in graduate school – learning in the context of relationship. That realization, in turn, introduced me to the very new experience of small groups.

By the midway point of his ministry, Jesus could have focused exclusively on large crowds. What pastor would not love that? But with the end in mind and a vision of a living church in his heart, Jesus wisely began to focus on a 'small group' of twelve disciples, most of whom became reproducing 'sent ones,' or apostles. In spite of the 'big crowd' mentality in today's church and the depersonalization of individuals in contemporary society, Jesus' strategy is still the right strategy.

That is why I so wholeheartedly recommend this book, *Small Group University*, to you. It is unusual to come across such a practical and useable tool for building small group discipleship dynamics into whatever kind of ministry you may be leading – all within the context of Spirit baptism and Spirit-filled living. Here, Brad Lewis writes out of his experience as both a pastoral practitioner and a spiritual mentor to thousands of young adults. In doing so, Brad gives us a wonderful gift from the Lord's heart, a road map for developing small group experiences that will personalize pastoral ministry and shape people's lives into life-time disciples of Christ.

–James Bradford
General Secretary
The General Council of the Assemblies of God

INTRODUCTION

As a child, I had my life figured out. I was going to attend college, major in animal agriculture, and work in the cattle breeding industry for the rest of my life. But even more than that, I really craved two things: intimacy and authenticity with God and people.

Christmas dinner when I was in seventh-grade was life-altering. I don't remember the food or the presents. But, I remember my cousin sharing about how she had been powerfully baptized in the Holy Spirit. As she told me about her encounter with God, my heart leaped out of my chest. I didn't know what she had, but I needed it!

Years later, I found myself in college as an animal science major. When Spring Break arrived, I went to my cousin's home for the entire week. I sat with her and her husband, clinging to every word as they spoke. It was the mentoring retreat of a lifetime. They taught me what it looked like to walk with God and how to intentionally love people.

Summer arrived, and I made a trek to Colorado to visit my uncle. Out of the blue, he asked, "Is it possible that you're called to full-time ministry?" In an instant, it hit me. I knew I was called. But, before the call to ministry would come to fruition, God had a lot more for me to learn.

Months later, I was baptized in the Holy Spirit. My life radically changed. I quickly became more bold, intentional, and loving. For the first time in my life, I cared more about others than I did about myself. I wanted what God wanted. My own dreams became secondary.

God was not done yet. A short time later, He powerfully touched me when I was reading the book of Hosea. In that book, God revealed truth that has changed my life to this day. In case you are unfamiliar with the book of Hosea, let me explain a little.

God had Hosea marry Gomer, a prostitute, so that he could experience the heartbreak of an unfaithful wife. Hosea was a prophet and served as God's mouthpiece to Israel. In experiencing the pain of having an unfaithful wife, Hosea could better identify with God. It was simple: Gomer wasn't faithful to Hosea in marriage, and God's people worshipped idols instead of Him. God's heart was broken.

Hosea's heart was broken. Through the storm, Hosea was able to have a glimpse of God's heart.

When I read this story, I felt God calling me to a deeper level of commitment. In response, I prayed a dangerous prayer. I asked God to give me a glimpse of his heart. Praying that prayer broke my heart for the lost and completely changed my approach to evangelism. Instead of targeting my friends, I began to ask God whose heart the Holy Spirit had been dealing with, and who was ready to receive Christ. I would walk into classes and ask God to point someone out. If He gave me a definite person, I would build a friendship as soon as possible. Frequently, I had the opportunity to lead that person to Christ. Having a glimpse of God's heart ensures that we will supernaturally love people instead of depending on our own human strength to love them.

Along with the revelation in Hosea, God gave me two verses in the book of 1 Thessalonians that became foundational for my life and ministry. In that book it states,

> *"But we proved to be gentle among you, as a nursing mother tenderly cares for her own children. Having so fond an affection for you, we were well-pleased to impart to you not only the gospel of God but also our own lives, because you had become very dear to us." —1 Thess. 2:7:8*

As a way to check my heart, the Lord guided me to place my name and the names of the people I minister to into this verse. So instead, it reads like this,

> *"But **Brad** proved to be gentle among **his college students**, as a nursing mother tenderly cares for her children. Having so fond an affection for the **college students**, **Brad** was well pleased to impart not only the gospel of God, but also **his very life** because **the students** had become dear to **Brad**."*

This reminded me to befriend and "do life" with others. God changed people from a project to a passion in my heart.

Shortly after graduating from college with a master's degree in quantitative genetics, God placed me in a part-time youth pastor position. I was ranching, pastoring, and working on theological training all at the same time. Finally, the day arrived when I resigned as president of my state cattle breeding organization, and I accepted the college ministry position that I have held since 1989. When I finally sold the last of my cattle, God exploded our ministry in the same month. It is amazing what God will do when you trust him fully.

Over 200 students I have pastored, mentored, and befriended have been called into full-time ministry. All from a secular college campus! I don't deserve all the fun I've had watching so many men and women answer the call of God on their lives.

One of my all-time favorite stories happened on a Sunday morning. An intern of mine wanted me to meet his mother after church. As I walked up to her, she burst into tears and said, "Thank you for loving my boys...thank you for hugging and mentoring my sons." She had sent two drug and alcohol-addicted young boys to college, but she got back a college pastor and a dynamic young man who has continued to be a person of influence. It doesn't get any better than that.

As I write this book, I am sitting in my cousin's house, looking at a beautiful river through the same window I looked out 37 years ago where the journey of this book began. This was the place where my cousin taught me the answer to my cravings. I have come to find we all share the same desire for intimacy and authenticity with God and others. Small group community is the answer to this desire. I hope you enjoy learning about it as we enter *Small Group University*.

CHAPTER 1

The Importance of a Ministry Goal

Some moments are never forgotten. Over 20 years ago, the college ministers in our community had come together for our usual fellowship time. After some discussion on general topics, one campus ministry staff shared the results of a recent survey by his ministry organization. He said, "we found that five years after college graduation, only about 20% of students who were in our ministry are still serving Jesus." The room became quiet. I was shocked. It was in that moment I thought, "God, if this is the best we can do, I'd rather go back to cattle ranching."

Life after graduation

I walked out of that meeting with a clear goal from God—to see everyone in my ministry serve God for a lifetime. But, what would that look like? How could I measure it? Five years after college graduation, I wanted each person to possess the following qualities:

1. *Serving in a Spirit-filled church*
2. *Thriving in a godly marriage (if married)*
3. *Raising godly children (if had kids)*
4. *Achieving financial stability*
5. *Influencing workplaces and neighbors for Jesus*

These five qualities became my one goal for every person.

How to get to the goal

The end goal needs to direct the current process. If I want to find people in a godly marriage, I should teach on healthy relationships. If people are going to have their finances in order, I need to talk about money. As a college pastor, I only have 30 weekly meetings each year. So, I must address the following six topics in my preaching to help them reach the goal:

1. *Dating and relationships*
2. *Leading a family*
3. *Relational evangelism*
4. *Responsibility with finances*
5. *The baptism in the Holy Spirit*
6. *Spiritual gifts in the marketplace*

—

Sermons are effective, but they are one-time events. I don't want God's message to end with my altar call. I want to keep the conversation going. My *monologue* ministry needs to team up with *dialogue* ministry. That's where small groups come in. When it comes to God's truth, people need to talk about it, hash it out, and see it in real life.

Large goals in small groups

It is important for the goals of small group to reflect the goals of the large group (or ministry at large). Consistency is key, and a unified direction is imperative. So, our small group leaders are trained and encouraged to cover the six topics listed above at strategic times during the year. This reinforces the topics with deeper discussion and greater vulnerability.

Having a ministry goal for your small group is key. It will determine what you talk about and keep you on track. Most importantly, it will help you make the disciples of Christ you want to see. What you do now will determine the result you get later. Effective discipleship requires two things: embracing the present and positioning for the future.

What is your ministry goal? Where do you want to see people in your small group five years from now? If you haven't written it down yet, you need to.

Don't lead without a goal.

Let your goal drive your ministry.

Write it down and live by it.

CHAPTER 2

THE PURPOSE OF A SMALL GROUP

There are countless people who would never darken the door of a church. However, many would be willing to attend a small group. I believe small groups are becoming the fastest growing mission field in America. Small groups reach the unreached and love the unloved in my city.

We have seen small groups *protect*, not *neglect*, the large group. In fact, the health of small groups will reflect the health of the large group. Frequently, more people in our ministry attend a small group during the week than our corporate worship services. Community is a valued resource.

If you observe a mother duck with her ducklings, one key element of teamwork is illustrated—unified direction. When the mother duck makes a turn, the ducklings are right on her tail… literally. When we all move in the same direction, the likelihood of success and survival dramatically increases. Groups may have different emphases and demographics, but all Christ-centered small groups should have the following five purposes in mind:

1. Meet the "small group need" in people's lives

We all need to feel a part of something bigger than ourselves. The large group (eg. church service) helps encourage Christians through corporate worship, prayer, and community. These are all necessary for growth. However, the large group has one major limitation—the ability to hide. People can go to church for decades, yet never develop a friendship nor confess a single sin. Even though they may be going through the most difficult seasons of their lives, they try to "be happy" and hide the pain. They leave just as hurt, broken, and alone as when they came.

People can hide in a large group, but they can't hide in a small group. The small group provides a safe place to ask questions, share personal "junk," and shed tears. Deep relationships are nurtured. Small groups eliminate hype and help people face reality, even when it hurts. The truth is, life has its challenges. In those moments, people need to be surrounded by others who will encourage them and pray for them. The "realness" of small group helps balance the "good times" experienced during corporate worship. This doesn't mean small groups aren't fun. Small groups simply provide a time to

"rejoice with those who rejoice, and weep with those who weep."
–Rom. 12:15

Small groups connect a big need to a big God.

2. Provide leadership opportunities

Bottom line—people need an opportunity to lead. Not everyone can be on the worship, hospitality, or technology team. For those of us who can't sing without giving a helpless bystander a migraine, this is good news! In the small group setting, all sorts of people (with varying talents) can develop their leadership skills in a low-pressure environment.

Allowing people to lead nurtures faithfulness and commitment in the group. It prevents people from developing a "Christian-party syndrome." Those who struggle with "CPS" all have the same symptoms. First, they attend the most exciting ministry (or "Christian party") in town. Then, when something bigger or better comes along, they "party-hop" to a different church gathering. If this attitude catches on in a ministry, people become inwardly focused and they no longer invite friends. Attendance drops. This is an emerging trap in many Christian movements. A leadership opportunity promotes faithfulness to a ministry and strengthens a sense of ownership.

3. Develop more leaders

Ultimately, small group is a training ground for future leaders.
At minimum, a group's co-leader should be learning to lead by
experience. The definition and value of co-leading are discussed later
in this book. In our ministry, we have had up to eight members of
a single group become small group leaders the following year. Small
group may start as a recovery center, but if it grows into a God-
ordained leadership academy, go with it!

Just like Paul had Timothy, leaders must have a person he or
she is mentoring, or "pouring into," as a future leader. The greatest
victory of leadership is being replicated or replaced by someone you
trained and personally discipled. Hopefully, someone else is doing
your job next year, so that together more people are reached for
Christ. Remember, training doesn't only happen in formal meetings.
People primarily learn by direct observation, or as we affectionately
call it: "osmosis." In other words, people learn best by simply being
with you. Remember, more is *caught* than *taught*. This form of
leadership training allows others to see you lead in daily life.

4. Pray for group and individual needs

In small group, maximal time can be dedicated to individual prayer
needs. The setting should be safe, private, and comfortable. Some
members will have never prayed out loud until attending small group.
In this case, offer a brief prayer tutorial. This should excite you--
people are leaving their comfort zone! Provide an atmosphere where
people can practice praying for each other without an enormous
audience. Need direction? Start with this encouragement: *Pray how
you wish someone would pray for you.*

Prayer needs will present themselves in a variety of forms. We
need to be ready. Stacy, an attendee of one of our women's small
groups, unexpectedly poured her heart out about her mother being
diagnosed with breast cancer. Instead of simply giving a hug and
saying "sorry," her small group leader said, "Let's pray right now!"
Stacy had a life-changing experience that night—all because she got
real, and her small group prayed.

It is so important that small groups meet people's needs. One of
the greatest ways to do this is giving the issue over to God in prayer.
We all have a choice. We can go on wishing an issue changes, or we

can storm the throne room of God in prayer for our brothers and sisters. The choice is yours.

5. Reach pre-Christians

Note that the term above is neither "heathens" nor "the lost." The way you view people will determine how you treat people. We always want to see the potential in others, just as Jesus "saw" the potential in Levi (Luke 5:27). The hope, of course, is to eventually drop the *pre-* in pre-Christian. Leaders must be reminded that small group is not a "bless me club" that remains inwardly focused. It is a group always looking for ways to incorporate others.

If you're a small group leader, here is a question for you: *Does your small group have a plan when a new person comes?* All established small group members must make newcomers feel welcomed and valued. Healthy groups have an emphasis both on relational evangelism and discipleship. In a later chapter, we will look in depth at how to make your small group more visitor friendly.

—

These five purposes are simple and essential, but frequently overlooked. They will provide direction for your small group at all times.

Determine your purpose.

Meet the need.

Get others involved.

CHAPTER 3

FACILITATING RELATIONSHIP

People ask, "Brad, what discipleship model do you use to see growth in your ministry?" After a chuckle, I say, "Well, I started hugging people 25 years ago!" Although it's not quite that simple, it isn't too far off. People can smell strategy a mile away, but they can't resist someone who genuinely loves them. Culture-shaking small groups are full of one thing—healthy relationships. Why complicate the issue? Loving people is a much simpler approach than any other discipleship model. It is also the most effective. The question becomes, "How do I facilitate those healthy relationships?" To jumpstart relationships in small group, a leader must include these four elements:

1. Be Transparent

No one will go deeper or be more vulnerable than you. Don't be deceived—we all have areas of past or present weakness. The more we share about our battles, the more others will share about their battles. The common misconception from leaders is, "I need to be the one who has it all together" or "everyone else needs my perfect example to inspire them." This could not be further from the truth. Leaders don't have to be perfect. But, they do need to be vulnerable. Statements like, "I struggled with purity" are not helpful. Nearly all of our leaders tell us that being specific about their own past or present struggles is the only way others will share specific weaknesses. Here is the reason this works: people will rarely identify with your victories, but they will always relate to your failures.

As a leader, the easiest way to promote vulnerability in the group is by sharing your "junk" first. Then ask, "do any of you love me any less now?" The obvious answer is "no." Why approach it this way? We have found that this conversation smashes Satan's lie that "if I share what's really going on, people will be disappointed in me." Truth sets people free.

> *"Therefore, confess your sins to one another, and pray for one another so that you may be healed." –James 5:16*

We have seen this promise to be true time and time again. Several years ago, Kate called her small group leader and said, "I can never see you again, I can't believe I shared what I did at small group last night. I have never told anybody those things, and I just met all of you!" Kate's leader assured her that small group was a safe place and no one thought any less of her. She kept coming to small group and today Kate is walking for God. When bondage is exposed, healing is imposed!

2. Help pre-Christians feel comfortable

Yes, Ezekiel did see a flying wheel in the air (Ezek. 1:15)—but don't talk about this on the first week of small group! I'm only half joking. Most believers who grew up in church don't detect the "Christianese" (language only familiar to discipled Christian people) gushing out of their mouth. Using terms such as "saved," "reformed theology," "Pentecost" or even "Old Testament" may be foreign to some. When you hear the phrase "the blood of the Lamb," a warm picture of Jesus' perfect sacrifice may enter your mind. A new person at small group, however, may be horrified and want to call a veterinarian. Use wisdom. Expect that newcomers did not grow up in church. If you use a term that not everyone may know, explain it.

Many people have never owned a Bible. Have a few extra on hand to give to newcomers. You'll help someone avoid embarrassment. When preparing the group to read a Scripture passage, give directions on where to find it (eg. Matthew is two-thirds of the way through the Bible and right before Mark). It's OK if everyone does not have the same version of the Bible. Use it to your advantage. Have one person read a verse from the New American Standard Bible and another read it from the King James version.

You'll uncover more meaning! Keep everyone up to speed. Remember, people's barriers are usually not *emotional*, they are *informational*.

3. Avoid divisive issues

There are several sensitive issues that should be avoided at all costs. Here is where your toes may get stepped on. Ready?

Don't talk about politics. Being a Republican or a Democrat has nothing to do with salvation. Also, don't talk about your vegetarian views, whether to approve of Wal-Mart shopping, stem cell research, or abortion. God's Word warns us about divisive issues. The potential of offending a newcomer outweighs the benefit of tossing around a divisive issue in small group. Discussing them individually outside of small group is the best way to handle them.

"Don't major on the minors" has become a common saying among our staff. Why turn someone off to God because of your political views? Here is the take home message: Focus on Christ, God's Word, and the Holy Spirit—other things will follow. If someone insists on discussing one of these issues, address them during a one-on-one. (We'll talk more about one-on-ones in Chapter 9.)

4. Don't go too deep too quickly

Every good learning experience starts with the basics. Small group is no different. Our staff agrees that a vast majority of leaders overestimate the theological knowledge necessary to lead a healthy group. In most circumstances, understanding the Gospel (Jesus' life, death, resurrection, and associated significance) and heart issues (eg. bitterness, impurity, loneliness, and unforgiveness) may provide enough content for 16 small group discussions.

Watching youth sports is intriguing. I am surprised at how a parent can scream at a second-grade basketball player from the stands, "Don't double dribble!" when the poor kid can hardly hold a basketball. The little kids are just excited to be out there! All the other parents are just grateful that their kids are burning off energy. Yes, I am all about training and feedback. But, expecting immediate biblical expertise from a new person leading small group is a recipe for disappointment. When it comes to intimacy with God, the joy is in the journey.

God's word encourages us, but confusion can bring about frustration and discouragement. This is why Paul writes to the Corinthians about first giving them spiritual milk instead of spiritual food (1 Cor. 3:2). Moving from Matthew to Revelation or from James to Song of Solomon is usually too big of a step. Make sure that your group is ready for solid food before giving it to them, or they won't know how to digest it and apply it to their lives. We will discuss a recommended flow of topics in Chapter 6 to illustrate this more effectively.

—

When these components are combined with a lot of prayer, high-fives, fist pounds, hugs, and plenty of hangout times, you have a great foundation for a relationship-rich small group.

Be real.

Slow down the pace.

Don't leave anyone behind!

CHAPTER 4

PRIORITIZING RELATIONSHIPS

You have likely heard the phrase, "time is money." Regardless of the amount, your income cannot buy you more than 24 hours a day. Most leaders know that meeting personally with others is essential to the discipleship process. However, you only have limited time to meet with people outside of small group. Instead of worrying, try following a great example. Jesus provided the best model for how leaders should prioritize their relationships.

Jesus' Priority Relationships

> *"And He appointed twelve, so that they would be with Him and that he could send them out to preach, and to have authority to cast out the demons." –Mark 3:14–15*

According to this passage, Jesus called the 12 disciples for three reasons. First and foremost, he called them to relationship with himself. Second, He sent them out to preach. Third, he called them to perform miracles and cast out demons. Relationship was one of the main reasons Jesus called the disciples.

Like it or not, the disciples were not treated equally. Peter, James, and John got more of Jesus' time and attention. Let's look at two specific examples in Scripture. Peter, James, and John were the only disciples that saw Jairus' daughter raised from the dead (Mark 5). They were also present when Jesus was transfigured on the mountain (Matthew 17).

More attention from Jesus yielded more fruitfulness in their future ministry. Peter and John drove the early church. They helped write the New Testament! We can assume that Jesus assessed leadership giftings within the group of 12 and gave more time to those with greater leadership potential. Shouldn't we do the same in our small groups?

Follow Jesus' Example

Your goal is to identify members capable of leading a group in the future. Then, spend most of your one-on-one time with them. (We'll talk more about how to identify future leaders in Chapter 10.)

What does this look like? Imagine you have 10 people in your group (including you and your co-leader). You only have two hours a week for one-on-ones. Each member has needs, but you want to invest the most time in future leaders. I have a one-on-one rotation method that will accomplish both. It will work for you and your co-leader!

Let's begin. You have eight people in your group. Conveniently, their names start with the letters A-H. Suppose Andy and Bob have significant leadership potential (underlined below). Use the following table to blaze out a three-week one-on-one strategy.

	You		Co-Leader	
	Hour 1	**Hour 2**	**Hour 1**	**Hour 2**
Week 1:	<u>Andy</u>	Chad	<u>Bob</u>	Dan
Week 2:	<u>Bob</u>	Everett	<u>Andy</u>	Frank
Week 3:	<u>Andy</u>	Garrett	<u>Bob</u>	Harry

Using the plan above, each person in your small group will meet with a leader every three weeks. However, the people with leadership potential (Andy and Bob) will have three meetings. This model will keep you from burnout and give you an opportunity to pour concentrated time into future leaders. Your time is valuable. Use it wisely.

Jesus discipled all 12 men, but He was most transparent with Peter, James, and John. Likewise, you must *pastor* the whole group but *mentor* future leaders. We will discuss characteristics of a mentoring relationship more in Chapter 12.

—

Prioritizing relationships will make the most of your spiritual and emotional resources. What's the result? New leaders will emerge. Do you prioritize your relationships?

Moses had Joshua.

Samuel had David.

Paul had Timothy.

Who will be your priority?

CHAPTER 5

How to Build a Group

A good carpenter has a strict method in building a house. Each part is constructed in a particular order. The foundation is poured, the structure is assembled, and the roof is attached. Then, cosmetic details of the house can be arranged. The experienced builder knows how to build a house in such a way that the process goes smoothly.

Great small groups are built with a plan. I am hopelessly practical. This doesn't mean I lack an appreciation for creativity, but I see great value in helping leaders streamline their efforts. Why make things harder than they have to be? After establishing a time and location to meet, we ask that leaders implement these four basic steps.

Establish a co-leader

Batman had Robin, Lucy had Ethel, Mario had Luigi, and Lewis had Clark. Although you may not be saving Gotham City or exploring the uncharted West, it's always good for someone to have your back!

Ninety-five percent of our small groups have a co-leader. We realize that small group models vary across the world, but we have found that groups with a co-leader are much less likely to fail. As a leader, it's easier to battle discouragement with a friend versus being alone. There are many ways to establish co-leaders, however, most ministries help pair leaders with co-leaders.

What is the definition of a co-leader? Rather than a one-sentence definition, let's paint a picture. A co-leader is the second person to talk or answer a question when discussion needs a boost. He or she is typically mentored by a small group leader and will become a new leader when new groups are added. If the leader can't make it to small group, the co-leader can fill-in. This person can also share the responsibilities of organization, invitation, and prayer. If a divisive issue arises, he or she is ready to support the leader.

2. Create a relaxed atmosphere

Don't give into the temptation. Although a coffee shop or other fun public place has curb appeal, these environments are destructive to the private atmosphere that makes a small group thrive. An apartment, home, or dorm room allows you to close the door. This is critical. When the door closes, people will feel more comfortable to share, pray, and cry (yes, even for those "tough guys"). These things happen readily when people know they won't be seen or heard by a curious passer-by!

Take the first five minutes to decompress. This is the time when you shoot the breeze. Ask how everyone's day was. People need a few moments to transition from their hectic day into a serious small group time. Have a question of the week for everyone to answer at the beginning of small group (eg. What was your favorite childhood Christmas gift?) Go around the room and share "highs and lows." This involves each person sharing the best and worst things that have happened during the week. Be flexible and pray if someone shares a deep hurt or weakness. A relaxed atmosphere will encourage others to open up. It will make them want to invite their friends to the next small group!

3. Invite! Invite! Invite!

We must make this truth crystal clear: Your church leadership and ministry website are not responsible for inviting people to your small group. Our small group leaders report that only one in 20 people will visit a small group because of an advertisement on a ministry website. Of our active small group members, over 80% of them will have two things in common:

1. *They were invited by another person in the group*

2. *They started coming within the first month of the small group's beginning*

What does this mean for a leader or co-leader? When attending church or a larger group service, meet people you don't know! Invite them to small group! I love hearing that a new person at church got invited to multiple small groups by different people. Remember, you would rather have someone get invited twice than not at all.

Other modes of invitation are also helpful. Personally messaging friends (eg. texting them) a couple days before small group is effective. This solidifies small group in their calendars before something else comes up. Here is an example of a great text invitation:

> "Hey John, this is Tim Jones. I met you Sunday morning and wanted to invite you to small group this Wednesday at 7pm! It is a fun time of guys getting together and sharing our lives. Would you ever like to come check it out? If you're free, I'd love to buy you coffee or soda beforehand, too! Let me know—hope your week is going well!"

Creating social media groups (eg. Facebook) and utilizing group apps (eg. GroupMe) are also helpful in the invitation process. Don't underestimate the power of a phone call. When in doubt, invite others via communication tools most utilized by them. Regardless of your method, personal invitation is a non-negotiable when it comes to building a group.

Pray! Pray! Pray!

"For our struggle is not against flesh and blood…" –Eph. 6:12

We must realize that our prayers are powerful and necessary. Popularity or charisma will only take a leader so far. Without prayer, the wheels are spinning but the car isn't moving. We encourage leaders to regularly pray for people in their small group. The most effective leaders are already praying for those who have not yet come! We believe God honors our specific prayers. When it pertains to small group, these specific prayers include asking God to open people's schedules for small group, provide a powerful anointing, and encourage people to bring friends.

God is always up to more than you think. You have no idea what God has already been speaking to people's hearts. He is the powerful and invisible builder of great things. The small group you lead may be the atmosphere God uses to transform a life, heal a hurt, or administer a blessing. There may be two people in your group or 22, but God has a plan for each one. Leave the results to Him.

Pray to build.

Invite to build.

Get help to build.

CHAPTER 6

THE TOPIC FLOW

A year of small group will likely endure the "hourglass effect." This phenomenon is also called "subjective acceleration"—the feeling that hits you when consecutive months seem to go by faster and faster. Eventually, you wonder, "where did this year go?"

Since there is limited time to discuss truth, pray for needs, and reach people for Christ, we have developed a proposed list of topics to cover throughout the year. Now, this is assuming that your small group will only last a year. Even if it lasts for more than a year, hopefully there are new people that join throughout your tenure. Therefore, this list can be used and recycled on a yearly basis to ensure that everyone has heard and learned about these concepts.

Our model is largely a "free market," meaning that we do not have a forced curriculum. However, we strongly recommend the following topic flow to each leader, which is incorporated in almost all of our groups.

Weeks 1-4: Building a Foundation

The objective in the first month is not to go deep, but instead to share lives. We have observed that people relatively new to Christ will only be able to go surface-deep in relationship with Him until these topics are addressed. The following are some great ideas for the first few weeks of small group:

Personal life stories

Go around the room and have each person share their life story. As a leader, you should go first to set the pace and spur vulnerability. We will teach you how to develop your personal testimony in Chapter 12.

Personal struggles/weaknesses

Sharing our "junk" from the past or present is a great way to break the ice. It establishes that we have all sinned and opens the door to restoration (James 5:16). Also, this precedent can permeate all future small group meetings. I would make sure that your group has built a decent level of trust before talking about personal struggles. But remember, vulnerability on the front end produces freedom on the back end.

Bitterness and Forgiveness

A majority of people in our small groups have struggled or are struggling in this area. Having a small group where you teach about forgiveness can be very effective. However, in order to maximize your effectiveness, be sure to provide a time when people can share areas of bitterness and unforgiveness in their lives. Then, help them pray through their problem. Once again, this increases the vulnerability level in the group. In Christ, forgiving is living. Don't get bitter, let Christ make you better!

Identity

Make sure your small group knows who they are in Christ. Someone in your group thinks he or she is worthless. God sees a precious treasure. Another relies on his or her appearance. God sees the heart.

Have a small group where you learn about what God thinks about us. For many, this will be one of the most encouraging and eye-opening moments of their lives. Encourage them to hold God's perspective close to their heart.

Sexual Integrity/Purity

Why does God hate sexual sin? He hates it because it hurts and destroys His beloved children. During this topic, you address issues such as pornography, masturbation, and sexual promiscuity. It is important to address the problem, but is also important to talk about a plan and solution. People must realize that God's freedom also comes with God's wisdom. Questions that should be answered include the following:

"What does God ask of us in the area of sexual integrity/purity?"

"I've messed up, can God really love and restore me?"

"What sources in my life (TV, cell phone, computer, iPad) need to be removed to be free?"

"What changes need to be made today?"

Redemption in these areas should be a primary focus. This can be a small group closely related to the one about sharing your junk. In today's world, we cannot skirt around this issue. Call it out of the closet. Attack these problems head on. Position people to be restored in Jesus' name!

Weeks 5-9: Solidifying Faith

People need to feel loved before they can be saved. Hopefully, you are ready as a group to explore the Gospel without resistance.

Specifics of Salvation and Jesus Christ

This is something that you should have ready for any small group. You never know when a new person is going to come. Giving them a chance to hear the gospel and respond to Christ is an incredible thing. Not only will their lives change, but everyone in your small group will know how to be evangelistic and attentive to the needs of pre-Christians. Without Jesus, small group wouldn't exist!

The Baptism in the Holy Spirit

We recommend a two-part series on this topic, as there is a lot of information to cover. Many times there are abundant questions. Taking two small groups to discuss the baptism in the Holy Spirit allows you to table more questions if you don't know the answer. It gives you the opportunity to retrieve additional information from God's Word, a pastor, or a ministry leader. It's OK to to say, "I don't know, but I'll get back to you," and follow up next time.

Of the two parts, the first can largely focus on who the Holy Spirit is and the role of the Holy Spirit. The second can target the baptism in the Holy Spirit. An in-depth teaching on this topic is discussed later in Chapter 15. These are subjects that are best described initially in the safe environment of small group, so a member is not surprised when they hear about it in a large group setting (eg. conference or retreat).

Weeks 9-12: Personal Growth

The purpose of this small group season is simple: Fully connect people to God instead of you. More than likely, you will not play an active role in each person's walk with the Lord for the rest of their lives. Therefore, you need to make sure they can be spiritually self-sustaining. In order to do this, be certain that your time together complements, not replaces, their consistent time with God in worship, His Word, and prayer.

Intimacy with the Lord

People will come into your small group with little to no knowledge of biblical worship or biblical prayer. Spending time teaching people the heart and meaning behind worship can be life-changing. Obviously, teaching people how to pray is an incredible necessity. Prayer should be a focus of every single small group.

Encouragement

We live in a society that is terrible at encouraging one another. It is much easier to tear each other down. Even as Christians, it is easy to be sarcastic and to poke fun at others. We rarely notice we are doing it. We verbally tear each other apart, despite what we see in the Bible. In Acts, the early church clearly encouraged one another daily. The Bible also says,

> *"Death and life are in the power of the tongue..."*
> *—Proverbs 18:21*

Teaching people the necessity of encouragement and how to effectively encourage others is a key component of small group. One of the most intimate times in small group is when we go around as a group and tell each other specific things that we love about each other. For this special time, we recommend at least an extra hour and a jumbo box of Kleenex. The time will be well spent! This activity is best introduced after deep-level relationships have been built.

Healthy same gender relationships

We live in a culture confused about what same gender relationships should look like. The Bible has several clear examples of healthy same gender relationships. They are powerful. We have much to learn from the relationships of David and Jonathan and of Ruth and Naomi. Use their stories when you talk about this subject. This is a topic that could also be shared at the beginning of a small group year to show the heart behind what a small group is supposed to be all about.

Weeks 13-beyond: Meet the need

Needs arise in life. We must address these real issues. These are needs that you observe within your group or are topics suggested by your group. I encourage you to ask your group if there are topics that they would like to study. Many of the following ideas are specific for certain age groups or situations, so don't feel obligated to cover any of them. They are just ideas. Because of this, we will not spend very much time on each subject.

Book Study or Life Study

When I say "book study," I don't mean taking a popular Christian book and studying it. I am talking about taking a book from the Bible and strategically walking through it. This type of book study is a great way to keep people engaged even when they are not in small group. It also allows them be prepared before showing up. It provides a way to show others how to study and harness wisdom from the Word of God. A great place to start is the book of James, as each verse in James is powerful and applicable. The book of James is also relatively short.

Another similar method is a life study. This is taking a look at a specific Bible character and studying their life. By studying the life of a biblical hero, we can learn from his or her successes and failures. We can learn about faithfulness from Joseph or repentance from David. There is so much we can glean from the characters in the Bible. In small group, God's Word is the ultimate Professor.

Dating and Relationships

This is a mandatory topic if you are leading a group of high school students, college students, or young adults. Teachings on purity, becoming the "right one," and having a God-centered relationship are crucial.

Faithfulness

Discuss the importance of this characteristic in marriage, family, friendship, and small group/church attendance! Faithfulness will affect them for the rest of their lives.

God's will

People generally have unrealistic expectations about discovering God's will. It is a historically difficult issue to navigate. A brief teaching can clear up a lot of confusion. Following God's desire leads to following God's will. We don't know God's specific will for people's lives. All we can really do is show them how to hear God's voice and receive direction from a biblical perspective.

Discovering gifts

We can help people understand their God-given gifts and help connect them to a ministry where their gifts can be used (eg. technology team, hospitality, children's ministry at church). This can be accomplished by encouraging people in areas of strength and talents in their life. Sometimes, people just need a little positivity and a little push.

—

This is not an all-encompassing list. If your topic flow works, you don't need to change it. This chapter can be a great starting point. If nothing else, it may stimulate good discussion on how to make adjustments if needed.

We recommend the use of short handouts. Handouts are usually a one-page summary of Scripture and main points of the small group topic. They are a great way to help people remember what they learned and have a "go-to" reference in the future. Several handout examples from our leaders are available for download at *XALeader.com/blog.*

The take home message is simple: position people to experience God and to grow with Him.

Meet people where they are at.

Be patient.

Take the journey together.

CHAPTER 7

ELIMINATING THE FEAR OF WEEK ONE

You prayed. You invited. Now you have a group of strangers in a room for small group. New people may base their entire perception of small group on the first week alone (sometimes within the first few minutes of being in the room). It is exciting that your new best friend could show up this week. With that in mind, you want to make the most of your first meeting.

In this chapter, I share 10 things that should be communicated to every small group member on week one. I also provide examples of what they need to hear from you. Keep in mind these have to be demonstrated whenever a new person comes to your group.

You are loved—I love you!

This is a brotherly or sisterly love. It's the way a good family loves each other—no strings attached. If no one in your life has ever told you they loved you, I'm happy to be the first.

I want to be your biggest fan

You might be a long way from home. I want you to feel like you have a "covering" if you would like one. You'll have big wins this year, and I want to celebrate them with you. On the flip side, if you catch a cold or need a trip to the emergency room, let me know. I want to do my best to be there for you.

I will respect your time

I won't make you stay forever at small group. I will have about an hour planned out, but after that, you're free to go. In fact, if you can only stay 15 minutes, come anyway. We'd love to pray for God's blessing on your life before you leave.

I want to help you find God's will for your life

By the end of this season of small group, my hope is that you will have better direction in your walk with God. I want to pray with you for your future. Whether it's finding a career or deciding on a new location for your life, I want God to take you in the right direction.

The rest of the week will be better because you came

I want you to see this time as an investment. You give an hour to God, and I believe He will honor that time. He will help you by making your relationships flow more smoothly, your work more efficient, and your challenges easier to handle.

I want to help you prepare for a Godly spouse (if you are seeking one)

If you are searching for a spouse, I want to help you become the right person rather than just find the right person. When you finally are ready to marry that "special someone," I want to be there praying for and supporting you the whole way.

There will be no secrets or surprises

God might surprise you, but I will not! If you bring a new friend, we don't have to talk about what I planned. We will have an audible ready so that your friend will feel comfortable and welcome during the discussion. I won't embarrass you or your friend. I only ask that you expect every week to be life-changing and allow God to surprise you with how much He moves in your life.

I will pray for you every day; I will pray with you at any hour

You can text or call me, and I will do my best to be available. Don't be afraid to call if you need prayer or if you're in trouble. I want to be someone you can rely on. Never feel like you are inconveniencing me.

We will use God's word as the "center post"

This won't be a small group that focuses on our own ideas. Whenever there is a question, we will go back to God's Word. Denominational backgrounds and theological debate will not be the focus, but rather we will focus on the fundamental truths in God's Word.

What is said here, STAYS HERE

Being in this small group means you agree to not share someone else's weakness to people outside the group. This is a safe place, and all of us will share things that are very sensitive. Keeping a confidence will be expected and respected.

—

Over time, we have noticed that people are retained better in small group when they know what to expect. If you only get one or two weeks with a person in small group, at least he or she will know your heart. A good first week can lead to a great year of small group. Remember, a first impression can only be made once. Following these steps will make others feel loved and appreciated. Nothing is more effective than getting started on the right foot.

Share your heart.

Eliminate the fear.

Hit a home run on week one.

CHAPTER 8

Group Dynamics

Making delicious food requires good cookware. It's one of the most important things I've discovered in my love for cooking. Small groups are no different. If you want great people, you need a great environment. Your small group's dynamic will make or break it's success. People want to *belong* before they *become*.

Discovering your group type

Nikki was one of my discouraged small group leaders. Well, discouraged would be a huge understatement. Her small group had dwindled to *just her and one other girl*. She felt like a failure. She came to my office to tell me she was done, finished.

"Why don't you invite Kinsey and Tracy?" I asked. "Better yet, ask one of them to host your small group!" Kinsey and Tracy had come to our large group meeting for the first time that week. Nikki thought I was crazy. I told her if it didn't work, she could throw in the towel.

Nikki called Kinsey the next day. "What do you do in small group?" Kinsey asked. Nikki explained that in small group, people do life together. "We share our struggles, read God's Word, pray for each other, and become great friends." She was shocked when Kinsey joyfully agreed to have the small group at her place! The small group grew to 12 people. Kinsey and Tracy still serve God today. These girls were looking for Nikki's group. Nikki simply had to step out in faith.

With the hundreds of small groups over the years, I've found that there are many types of groups. Each one is a little different. Each one has unique strengths. I embrace it, because everyone has different needs. Some people fit well into one group but not another. I want every small group to incorporate God's Word and have a relational emphasis. After that, group dynamics can take over. Your small group may be one of the following types.

1. *Relational*

2. *Bible study*

3. *Topical*

4. *Book study*

5. *Accountability*

6. *Prayer*

A group should operate in most of these at some point. But ultimately, each will prioritize one. Some groups love walking through a Christian book together. Others may focus on prayer and intercession. Nikki's small group read God's Word, prayed, and had accountability each week. It was still definitely a *relational* small group. Sharing life and becoming best friends was the overall theme.

What type of group is yours? What do you want it to be? If you know your small group type, you will have less confusion and more direction. If you know what your group brings to the table, you'll want to talk about your group and share it with others.

Destructive Assumptions

Let's take a look at a little scenario:

You: *"Want to come to my Bible study?"*

Your friend: *[Long pause]*

Your friend's thoughts: *"Do they sit in a dark room and hum? Sing Kumbaya? I don't know anything about the Bible!"*

This is what people may think when you invite them to a "Bible study." Do we fully support Bible reading? Absolutely. Do we avoid the term to be more "relevant?" Absolutely not. We intentionally call our gatherings *small groups* and not "Bible studies" to embrace other aspects of discipleship. And, it's a lot less scary, don't you think?

Don't make assumptions. Not everyone knows where Leviticus is in the Bible. If you are invitational, you'll notice that most people won't even bring a Bible. Always have a few extra Bibles on hand. Be willing to give them away. Bibles make the best gifts and will keep someone from feeling embarrassed.

Some people believe men and women speak different languages. We don't have nearly enough time to explore that topic in this book, but I can assure you that speaking "Christianese" will destroy your group. Never assume people know Christian terms. Saying "small group" instead of "Bible study" is just the beginning. Start listening to yourself. Keep a language inventory. Select suitable alternatives that everyone will understand. The list of Christianese terms is endless, but here are a few:

Life story vs. testimony

"Tell me your testimony!"

To a pre-Christian, you may have just elicited a mental picture of Judge Judy. Don't go there. Everyone has a life story. Pre-Christians don't have a testimony yet. To a person who hasn't been to church in a while, testimony is only a legal term. That's why it is best to go around the room and share life stories instead!

Avoid "saved"

"Saved from what?"

If I hadn't been around Christian circles before, this is what I would think. Instead, talk about how you started a personal relationship with Jesus and accepted his love and forgiveness.

How to Handle Prayer

Christ-centered small groups fall in one of two categories: those who pray, and those who stray. I believe small group is the best place to receive prayer and to pray for others. God's Word makes it clear that praying for each other is powerful and effective (James 5:16). However, there is a right and wrong way to get your group praying.

Asking everyone to pray out loud during the first week is the wrong way to handle prayer. Would you be expected to play a Mozart concerto at your first piano recital? No way! Praying out loud is just as intimidating.

Splitting up and praying in pairs (or very small groups) is the right way to start praying in a group. Have the pairs exchange prayer requests and pray for one another. This is simple and non-threatening!

If someone shares a deep hurt or serious need with the group, collective prayer is an excellent next step. At this point, consider putting them in what I call the "hot seat." This involves gently leading the group to into a time of prayer. Then, follow the prompting of the Holy Spirit. Let's take a moment to briefly illustrate the "hot seat."

You are in small group and Jim just shared that his sister was diagnosed with cancer. He starts to weep. Now is the time for the hot seat! Have Jim sit in the middle of the circle. Tell Jim what you're going to do and why. You can take a moment to educate the group on how prayer with the laying on of hands is biblical and demonstrated in the early church (Acts 8:17, 9:17, 13:3, 19:6, 28:8). Have everyone in the group gently lay their hands on him. Then, open in prayer and ask others to pray out loud over Jim as well. If the group isn't accustomed to praying out loud, you may have to ask specific people to pray. Have one person pray at a time, in orderly fashion. That is the "hot seat."

Sometime during the year, I encourage you to take a whole small group and pray for every person using the hot seat method! God has done major feats in hot seats!

That group has issues!

People aren't perfect. In fact, most are far from it! If you are inviting people without discrimination (just as Jesus would), you need to expect *issues*. Issues only reinforce the truth that we need Jesus! For better or worse, social ones are the most noticeable. If you lead small groups long enough, you will be able to identify specific people who define these issues. If you can't think of someone, that someone might be you!

The Joker

"Hey guys! Look at Travis' shorts! It's the middle of winter man!"

"Bro, let's arm wrestle, your arms are so big and you would totally beat me!"

The Talker

"More people should be in the military. The army is, of course, the toughest place to be. But, it's the price for freedom. We just don't have enough emphasis on what is important anymore. I just have to say this to get it off my chest..."

The Know-it-all (these are everyone's favorite)

"I'll send you all links of this great new megachurch podcast I found. I'm really into podcasts, blogs, and new books. Hey, just so you all can pray for me, I feel called to preach to thousands of people and be famous."

The Negative Nelly

"I hate my job. The people I work with are lazy and my boss is a so stupid."

The Shy guy (or girl, it just didn't rhyme)

[Silence]

The Dramatic

"I know I said this last week, but this was really the worst week ever. Well, yesterday was great, but today was horrible."

"You won't believe what Vanessa said to me. I just wanted to throw something, you know!? She thinks she is really something with her boyfriend."

—

These examples are as serious as they are humorous. Issues must be addressed quickly, because they have the capacity to sink your group. Someone who jokes around during small group will disable intimate conversation. The talker or the dramatic will steal the show and drown out the shy guy. The know-it-all or negative Nelly will cast doubt on spiritual truth. I get nervous just writing about it.

Do you have someone like this in your group? If not, you will. Keep your cool. The good news is, it can be managed. There is an honest way to confront the issue without degrading the person. If you have a person with one of the traits above, first, redirect the conversation while in front of the group. Next, talk to the individual one-on-one after small group. This avoids embarrassment.

The Kingdom of God operates under authority. A small group leader is an extension of God's authority and the lead pastor's authority. At the end of the day, you are the leader God positioned in the small group. It is your job to keep the group on track. Give your talkers a job in small group. Have them ask the shy people questions to get them involved. Remind them that if there are eight people in the group, they can only say two things the entire time. Tell the dramatics and jokers to plan a post-small group hangout and save their comments until then. If a know-it-all opens a theological debate, tell them that you can discuss it together later in the week. If you step out, God will step in. If you initiate, God will help officiate!

Don't make assumptions.

Involve Christ in the crisis.

Tackle personal growth issues.

God will honor your efforts.

CHAPTER 9

THE ONE-ON-ONE

Justin was the typical rebellious church kid. He thought he had it all: women, alcohol, and drugs. But, nothing satisfied. Feeling hopeless and depressed, he called his mother and told her how sick of his lifestyle he was. She suggested he make an appointment with me.

Justin later told me, "I stood outside your door for what seemed like an eternity, fully expecting judgment and rebuke from you, because you were a pastor." Continuing, he said, "When I sat down on your couch, you smiled at me and asked me to share my story. I couldn't believe what happened next. As I burst into tears, all the hurt, junk, and sin came spilling out of my mouth. Still expecting the worst, I couldn't believe it when you sat down beside me, put your arm around me, and said, *'Justin, I care about you and Jesus is going to change everything.'* That day changed my life."

Justin's life was changed by an important ministry tool: the one-on-one. One-on-one's are simply that. One-on-one. It's time for you to do life together. Things are accomplished in this setting that will never happen in a group setting. Don't do a one-on-one without the One who can really make a difference!

One-on-one ministry is the key building block of relational ministry. People feel loved and welcomed when someone in leadership invests in them. Future leaders are identified and developed in the one-on-one setting. It is a time for spiritual impartation, vulnerability, and life-changing prayer. Peak communication and relational experiences happen during one-on-ones.

Why One-on-ones?

If you're a small group leader, you must ask yourself a simple question: Does your small group attract people?

We live in a culture that battles for attention like never before. The latest trends, fashions, and events draw people in and drown out everything else. So, what will make your small group stand out? How will you make it attractive? Unlike pop culture, it's not more hype. It's one-on-ones. Having one-on-ones with your small group members gives them special attention. It adds value to their lives. People crave this connection. Plain and simple. It takes time, but it is worth it.

Michael had what it took to be a great small group leader. He was personable and had a lot of biblical wisdom. He took extra time to prepare a great lesson every week. Yet, Michael approached me and was very confused. "Why isn't my small group growing?" He felt like he was doing everything right, yet guys weren't coming. The guys he had were rarely there. I simply asked him, "How often do you meet with your guys one-one-one?" He looked at me with a tilted eyebrow and said, "Why? What does that have to do with it?" My answer was again very simple. "Everything, Michael, everything."

We can be doing everything right, but without going out of our way to meet with people, we are falling short. People can come every week but never feel connected, simply because they don't know the leader. They don't feel important to the leader. Most importantly, they don't feel like their leader sees them as a friend. A common of error of small group leaders is to allow their title or position in the small group disconnect them from the people in their group. If you feel superior, you need a holy heart check. Small group leading is a passion, not a position.

Managers communicate, but leaders connect. One-on-ones make a person feel connected to the leader. If there is one thing I've learned about ministry, everyone wants to be connected to the top. It is just how we are wired. Not only that, but a one-on-one deepens the relationship. It gives an opportunity to address individual needs and provide in-depth explanations. The following types of ministry are best done in a one-on-one setting:

1. *"Getting to know you"*

2. *Ministering salvation*

3. *Praying to receive the baptism in the Holy Spirit*

4.   *Dealing with a problem*
5.   *Imparting wisdom and advice*
6.   *Developing leadership skills*

Location

For vacations, my wife, Kay, loves to travel to far-away places. I prefer to stay near home or spend the weekend together at a nearby bed and breakfast. Although I see the value in both preferences, the locations come with very different expectations and goals. Kay may want to visit a famous Presidential monument, but I might want to read a good book and go for a walk. Since famous monuments are hard to come by in North Dakota, we need to choose a vacation destination that provides mutual enjoyment. Likewise, there are advantages and disadvantages to every one-on-one location. The right location can put a gust of wind in your sails. The wrong location can make you feel like you're walking the plank!

A one-on-one can take place in many different locations. I have had one-on-one meetings in my office, at my home, in a student's dorm room, at a coffee shop, at a restaurant, and in a barn. This list doesn't even scratch the surface. My point is, there are a lot of places to have a one-on-one, but they don't all produce the same result. I largely prefer meeting students in my office or my home. Restaurants aren't the best for me. I think the reason is obvious. There is food involved and I get distracted!

We will take a look at a few options. I have broken them down into three categories: *your turf, a neutral zone,* and *their turf.* Let's take a look:

Your turf

I love meeting people in my office or at my home. There is privacy, it's my turf, and I have access to resources if I need them. The couch in my office has been affectionately named "The Crying Couch." The privacy of my office allows people to feel comfortable being open and vulnerable. However, there are drawbacks to meeting in my office. It is several miles away from where many of the people in my ministry live. If they don't have a vehicle, it can be inconvenient to meet there. A person can also feel threatened by meeting a pastor at a church office. They may also feel uncomfortable meeting someone they don't know very well at their home.

A neutral zone

This is anywhere that is common ground for both people involved. Coffee shops, restaurants, and parks are fit into this category. These places are all convenient, public, and safe. However, there is a downside to the neutral zone. One problem with coffee shops and restaurants is that they cost money. The biggest barrier in these public venues is that people will often not feel comfortable sharing about deep or vulnerable issues. Your time has the tendency to get filled with cliché conversation and you often leave discouraged, feeling like you didn't gain any ground with your group member. If you meet in a neutral location, be aware of these challenges to avoid pitfalls and maximize your time.

Their turf

These locations are "home" for the person you are meeting with. A person's house, apartment, or dorm room is private and convenient for that person. He or she may feel the most at ease at home, but this location still has challenges. A person may have distracting posters, people, or pets at his or her place. This can restrict conversation and crush vulnerability.

All locations have their advantages and disadvantages. Ultimately, choose the location best fitted for the type of conversation you want to have. There will be times where a coffee shop is a great place and you can accomplish what needs to be accomplished. There will also be times that "The Crying Couch" is the only place someone needs to be. You, as a leader, need to be the judge of what is best.

One-on-one "how to" guide

So you've made it to a one-one-one, now what? If nothing else, offer love and relationship. *People don't care how much you know until they know how much you care.* Don't come across like a therapist. You're making a best friend.

Be a good listener

Can you think of someone in your life that talks all the time, but rarely listens? Is he or she fun to talk to? Of course not. Now, can you think of someone who is a great listener? You probably have a smile on your face now. Being a good listener is being a good leader. I encourage you to sit close. Don't sit behind a desk. If you're getting to know someone (what I call a "get-to-know you"), always start by saying, "Tell me your life story. You were born, and then what happened?" People love talking about themselves. It shows you're interested in them. Keep asking questions to direct the conversation.

Be transparent

Remember, no one will go deeper in vulnerability than you do as a leader. When you share your junk, it frees them to share theirs. Ask them what they struggle with or need prayer for, but before you do that, share your struggles. They will feel much more comfortable after that. Why? Because they know you.

Pray to be used in gifts of the Holy Spirit

The truth is, the Holy Spirit is a much better small group leader than I ever will be. Each person you meet with has specific needs, and the Holy Spirit knows them all. He distributes gifts to meet the need of the moment and for the common good (1 Cor. 12:7). Pray that God gives you a specific message to share. We will talk more about being used in gifts of the Holy Spirit in Chapter 16.

Use time wisely

People are busy. Work happens. School happens. Relationships happen. It is important that you honor the person's time when you meet with them. I would never want someone to leave my office feeling like his or her time was wasted. Leave them wanting more. If they wish they were painting a barn with a toothbrush…you might need to rethink your use of one-on-one time. Before you enter a one-on-one, think and pray about what questions you should ask.

Avoid small talk

This isn't the time to discuss the latest in sports, weather, or media. Talking about these things may be a great way to break the ice, but don't linger on them. Unfortunately, a majority of people's conversations end with cliché conversation. Break the mold. Deep down, we are all longing for deep relationships. People will be thankful when they realize you care more about them than you do the current baseball scores.

Don't rush

Are you looking at your watch or cellphone? If you have to, set aside more time than you need or just communicate how much time you have available. This way, no one will feel rushed.

Keep the conversation on track

Some people beat around the bush until there is a worn foot path! Don't get caught in the fringes. Great small group leaders are crucial conversation specialists. It is common for a person to avoid difficult conversations. People will change the subject when they feel uncomfortable. Press on, because you are likely nearing the place in the conversation where they need spiritual breakthrough.

Always pray together

More than a deep conversation, people need prayer. Even if it was the worst one-on-one in small group leader history, God is still able to move powerfully as you end in prayer. Prayer is supernatural. It is *super* because God is involved. It's *natural* because you are involved. Each person needs a touch from God. If you are in a public setting, this can be done quietly and discretely, but always remember that it is very important. If you're meeting with someone of the same gender, hold hands or put a hand on the person's shoulder if it's appropriate. As a safe rule, avoid touching while praying with someone of the opposite gender, as that could confuse intentions.

Sometimes a one-on-one is a seed, and you won't see the fruit. Sometimes it was step 11 of a 324-step process that God wants to use to provide a miracle in someone's life. Keep praying, and let God move.

—

One-on-ones have accounted for some of the greatest stories in our ministry. Mandy's story is a great example. Mandy was new to small group. When her small group leader asked her to meet up to get to know her, she was amazed. She had met several Christians, but she always felt like they didn't care about her. At the end of the one-on-one, her small group leader asked if it was ok to pray with her. With tears in her eyes, Mandy said, "no Christian has ever asked to pray with me." Mandy's life changed that day. Pray with people you meet with.

Be an encourager. People are emotionally torn apart by the people closest to them. That is just what happens. Simply complimenting a person will make them feel loved. In most cases, giving a hug before you depart is the best way to close a one-on-one.

It is important to follow the leading of the Holy Spirit in these meetings. Use the one-on-one opportunity to love people, impart vision, encourage, exhort, plant the Word in their hearts, and share your life experiences with them.

People want your friendship.

People want to see who you really are.

People want a one-on-one with you.

CHAPTER 10

HOW TO IDENTIFY FUTURE LEADERS

Great leaders produce new leaders. This reproductive process is critical in small groups. In order to grow the number of small groups in your ministry, the number of leaders must increase. The best future small group leaders are developed in *existing small groups*. But, how can you tell if someone will make a good leader before they become one? You have to learn to identify those with leadership potential. In this chapter, I'll teach you how to do it with the help of the Holy Spirit.

Not everyone in small group will be capable of leading a group of his or her own. That is perfectly OK. Some small groups will have several potential leaders, while others will not. People are at different places emotionally and spiritually. It is the small group leader's role to follow the leading of the Holy Spirit when it comes to identifying future leaders. It's not all about finding the most talented people. It's about finding the right people. Setting a right person up to be a new leader is one of the best things a current small group leader can do.

The right thing at the wrong time is still the wrong thing. Setting a wrong person up, or the right person before they are ready, can be detrimental. So who would be *right* for being a new small group leader? In other words, who has leadership potential?

We look for the stars. You are probably thinking, "Wait, I thought he said you aren't just looking for the most talented people?" You are absolutely correct. The STAR Principle is easy to remember and will help you identify future leaders. You want to look for people that are:

Spirit-led

Teachable

Available

Reliable

These are the *true* STARs.

Spirit-led

Without a doubt, a future leader must be sensitive to the Holy Spirit. A leader is entrusted with the spiritual growth of others. That is quite the responsibility! The Holy Spirit is much more capable to lead a small group than you or I ever will be. A spirit-led leader always trusts the voice of the Holy Spirit over his or her own voice.

When identifying future leaders, it is important to ask them where they are at with the Holy Spirit. Are they open to the baptism in the Holy Spirit? Are they eager to walk in the incredible gifts available to them through the Holy Spirit? We will discuss the baptism of the Holy Spirit and Spiritual gifts in chapters 15 and 16.

It was evident that Nicole had leadership potential. When she encountered Jesus Christ as a college student, this potential was made accessible for the Kingdom. She subsequently experienced the presence and power of the Holy Spirit in her life. When she became a small group leader, she felt inadequate and unprepared. Over the next year, the Lord blew her away. As she remained sensitive to the Holy Spirit, she began to operate in the *word of knowledge*, and girls in her life were supernaturally blessed! Nicole was a good leader, but when she allowed the Holy Spirit to lead her, supernatural ministry resulted. Holy Spirit empowerment augments a person's leadership potential.

Teachable

A future leader is teachable, not perfect. Ideal leaders realize that they have not "arrived." They are hungry to learn and grow. When seeking future leaders, look for the people who are eager to be challenged and pushed to the next place in their relationship with Christ.

What do teachable people look like? They ask questions. They want to be mentored. When they mess up, they get back up and learn from their mistakes. They have a desire to learn from wisdom, not consequences. They begin to learn from *others'* mistakes.

A key component of small group discipleship is lovingly pointing out areas of sin that need correction and leading the person toward Jesus for freedom. A teachable person will respond by taking serious and firm steps to walk in victory. They stay consistent with accountability. They are vulnerable and are thankful when a mentor is willing to ask the tough questions (eg. are you remaining sexually pure?)

I love Zach's story. Zach got involved in a small group. He had rough edges. He was in a compromising relationship and had a quick temper. From the outside, Zach would not have looked like a potential leader. His small group leader saw something else. Zach asked many spiritual questions. When his small group leader would suggest he do something to walk in more obedience to Christ, he did it quickly. He asked his small group leader to hold him accountable. Over the next couple of years, Zach became an effective small group leader, impacting many lives for Christ. Leadership potential is proportional to teachability.

Available

Another quality to look for in a *STAR* is availability. These are the people that are consistent. Servanthood is fun for them. They drop anything if a friend is in need. The goal is to make small group leaders go-to people in the lives of others, but people don't become leaders if they don't have the time to lead! Everyone is busy to some degree. But when trying to identify leadership potential, seek out those who make time in their schedule for you and for the things of the ministry.

Being an available leader is often overlooked and underappreciated. Someone in the group will need to talk at an inconvenient time. They will lose a family member. There will be an accident. They will be in a situation where they feel they have nowhere else to turn. Can they turn to the leader?

Jeff had a young man named Pete in his small group. He was beginning to grow spiritually. Pete was serving God for the first time in years. One night, Jeff got a phone call that would shape him as a leader forever. Pete had put himself in a bad position and was arrested for possession of marijuana. He felt like he had no one to call…except Jeff. Jeff was there for Pete when no one else was. Over the next several months, Jeff walked with Pete through this muddy moment in his life. It was dirty. But, it was worth it. They both became better men and better friends. Who in your group is available? They may make great leaders.

Reliable

The final quality to look for in a *STAR* is reliability. Reliable people are loyal. You can count on them. A future leader must be faithful to not only small group, but to you, your ministry, and most importantly, his or her relationship with Jesus Christ. One reliable leader is worth more than 10 talented, but unreliable, leaders.

When it comes to leadership, reliability trumps talent. Lisa would not have been voted "Most Likely To Lead." She was a back row kind of girl. She didn't draw attention to herself. In small group, she wasn't the most talented or the most spiritual. But, her small group leader considered her the most reliable member. She was always there. She was an excellent friend. When asked to lead a new small group, she declined. Later, she had a life-changing encounter with the Holy Spirit and decided to give leading a try. She eventually became one of the greatest small group leaders I have ever known. Without delay, she raised up some of the most effective leaders in our ministry. Reliability is key.

Remember the *STAR Principle* as you seek out those with leadership potential. Keep your eyes open for spirit-led, teachable, available, and reliable people. Here are a few other questions you can ask when trying to identify future leaders:

- *Are they consistent in their time with Jesus every day?*
- *Are they outwardly focused with an invitational heart?*
- *Where are they at with the baptism in the Holy Spirit? Are they seeking it? Are they walking in it?*
- *Are they vulnerable and open with you and the group?*
- *Do they desire purity and pursue it?*
- *Who do they spend a majority of their time with?*

—

The role of the Holy Spirit in identifying future leaders cannot be overemphasized. The *STAR Principle* is only effective when the Holy Spirit is involved. Ask Him to highlight future leaders in your heart. He is the best identifier of them.

Mentoring makes your spiritual ceiling become someone else's spiritual floor. Your goal is to produce better small group leaders than you. Not everyone in your group will lead a group someday, but pray someone will!

Identify new leaders.

Cast vision and replicate yourself.

If you don't, no one else will.

CHAPTER 11

DEVELOPING AN EFFECTIVE TESTIMONY

A testimony beats an argument every time. Sharing your testimony, or life story, is one of the most powerful ways to communicate the power of God. People can deny the Bible and Jesus if they choose to, but they can't argue with the evidence of a changed life.

As a small group leader, you need to know the correct way to share a life story, teaching others to do the same. A common mistake is talking too much about what your life was like before Christ. Don't spend 95% of the time describing how bad your sinful life was and then, at the very end, say, "And then I met Jesus and everything has been great ever since." Although it is important to tell people where you came from, telling others what Christ has done in your life is more important. In this chapter, I'll walk you through the components of an effective testimony.

Components of an Effective Testimony

Specific events that led to salvation

First, briefly share about your life before Christ. When describing the events, highlight how they eventually pointed you to Jesus. Be careful not to draw attention to sin, but to how much you needed a Savior.

Don't try to out-do another person's testimony by exaggerating your sin or stretching the truth. Be vulnerable, concise, and wise when sharing details with certain people. Some audiences may be able to handle more than others (eg. specific purity struggles).

Just because you weren't in jail or you have never partied doesn't mean you have a lame testimony. Give praise to God for sparing you from those things. We all need Jesus equally,

> *"For all have sinned and fall short of the glory of God"*
> —Rom. 3:23

Your life before becoming a Christ-follower should take 20% of your story. The other 80% should involve your salvation experience and life change. With that in mind, don't try to cater to everyone. Expect the impact of your testimony to be greatest on those who had similar past experiences.

The salvation experience

Jesus is the hero of every testimony. I cringe when I hear testimonies that end with a long tribute to someone's mom who was praying for them or a friend who brought them to church. Think about your audience. Someone listening may have a mom who hurt them. Some may feel like they have no friends. If Jesus isn't the hero, people will leave thinking, "Well, I wish my mom loved me that much" or "it would be nice to have friends who cared about me." When you lift up the name of Jesus, the furthest heart is ready to receive His love and power.

Explain the events that led you to becoming a Christ-follower. A lot of people believe in God, so don't stop there. Use Jesus' name! Talk about the experiences that drew you closer to Him. Don't worry if you can't remember all the specifics. If nothing else, be sure to include that you made a decision to make Christ your Lord and Savior. This is what you want others to do! Share as many details as possible.

Life change

Share how your life changed after Christ became a part of it! If you don't, you'll leave people thinking, "So what?" Give others a glimpse into your relationship with Jesus. Talk about how He's helped you overcome sin, act in boldness, and stay encouraged! What is special to you will be special to others. Don't forget to describe ways Jesus has *used* you after committing your life to Him.

Current growth

Tell people what God is currently doing in your life. It's OK to share about the sin Jesus is still helping you overcome. A relationship with Christ is an ongoing process. When you share how you're currently growing, you emphasize that God's not done with you. Accepting Christ is not a one-time event. It's a lifetime decision.

More Winning Tips for Sharing Your Testimony

Sharing a good life story requires preparation. You should be able to share three different versions of your testimony: A one-minute, a five-minute, and a 20-minute version. Then, no matter how much time you have, you can tell a great story.

Have you ever heard a 20-minute testimony when you only had five minutes to listen? It can ruin its effectiveness! Know what situations are best for each version of your testimony.

A one-minute version works great anytime. A five-minute version is most suitable for the small group setting. You can focus on all the main points without giving all the details. Your 20-minute version is excellent for deep conversations and during one-on-ones. Share it when getting to know someone on a deeper level.

Take time to develop an effective testimony. Coach others to do the same, because every testimony has overcoming power:

> "And they overcame him by the blood of the Lamb, and by the word of their testimony; and they loved not their lives unto the death." –Rev. 12:11

Sharing your testimony is best when spoken to the right person, in the right way, at the right time. After hearing your story, people will discover what God is capable of doing. Your testimony is a prophecy that God can do it again.

Believe that your story will bring people into relationship with Christ.

The cross is not a decoration, it's a proclamation and a demonstration!

Jesus Christ has victory—He won!

CHAPTER 12

CHARACTERISTICS OF A MENTORING RELATIONSHIP

How do you view the world? I think the Grand Canyon is huge. An ant thinks a leaf is huge. How can both be true?

It all depends on how you define "huge." If you want to be accurate, you can't use words loosely.

One word that is used far too loosely in our culture is the term "mentoring."

How do you know if mentoring is really happening?

Let's look into God's Word.

Second Timothy is the mentoring manual of the Bible. This is Paul's last letter, written shortly before his impending death. The letter is unique in that Paul wrote mostly from his heart, not his head. Paul didn't write to just anyone. He wrote to Timothy, his spiritual son, who would carry on his legacy (2 Tim. 1:2). Paul's final words of encouragement have echoed throughout generations and provide key principles for us today.

Like a Cadillac among bicycles, mentoring relationships are distinct from others. In Second Timothy, there are nine identifiable characteristics that illustrate a mentoring relationship. If any of these characteristics are missing, mentoring is not reaching its full potential. Mentoring always takes place in the context of relationship, not curriculum.

Let's take a look at the nine characteristics of a mentoring relationship:

1. There is a heart connection

> *"To Timothy, my beloved son: Grace, mercy and peace from God the Father and Christ Jesus our Lord. I thank God, whom I serve with a clear conscience the way my forefathers did, as I constantly remember you in my prayers night and day, longing to see you, even as I recall your tears, so that I may be filled with joy." –2 Tim. 1:2-4*

In order for mentoring to take place, there needs to be spiritual chemistry between the mentor and mentee. Notice the tender words Paul uses in the above verses. Timothy was not just another visitor. For Paul, seeing Timothy was like a soldier being reunited with family after serving overseas. When mentoring is happening, both people are excited for the next time together.

2. Anointing is imparted

> *"For this reason I remind you to kindle afresh the gift of God which is in you through the laying on of my hands.... Guard, through the Holy Spirit who dwells in us, the treasure which has been entrusted to you." –2 Tim. 1:6, 14*

Every mentor wants to pass on their gifts, wisdom, and anointing to the next generation. The ultimate goal is the mentee accomplishing more than the mentor. Mentees can receive supernatural benefits from their mentor's established walk with Jesus over a very short time. Passing on the anointing and blessing of God must be a priority. As a mentor, what you pass is what will last.

3. A son becomes a father / a daughter becomes a mother

> *"You therefore, my son, be strong in the grace that is in Christ Jesus. The things which you have heard from me in the presence of many witnesses, entrust these to faithful men who will be able to teach others also." –2 Tim. 2:1–2*

My staff knows almost everything I know. I have taught them a lot, but I had to be the learner first. When it comes to ministry wisdom, learn it, then guard it. When faithful people emerge, pour it out! Paul also instructs us to mentor faithful people who are able to teach others. Faithfulness and leadership potential are established triggers to initiate a mentoring relationship.

4. God's Word is handled accurately

"Be diligent to present yourself approved to God as a workman who does not need to be ashamed, accurately handling the word of truth." –2 Tim. 2:15

Growing up on a farm with livestock and machinery taught me the importance of one essential skill: appropriate handling. Standing in front of spooked livestock can result in serious injuries. Carelessness around heavy machinery could mean a trip to the emergency room. Why would we treat God's Word with any less respect?

God's word is a treasure that requires accurate handling. Sadly, some have manipulated and misled sincere followers by twisting Scripture. God's approval rests on our ability to accurately present His Word.

5. Priorities are in order

"Now flee from youthful lusts and pursue righteousness, faith, love and peace, with those who call on the Lord from a pure heart. But refuse foolish and ignorant speculations, knowing that they produce quarrels. The Lord's bond-servant must not be quarrelsome, but be kind to all, able to teach, patient when wronged, with gentleness correcting those who are in opposition, if perhaps God may grant them repentance leading to the knowledge of the truth." –2 Tim. 2:22–25

Mentors warn against destructive behavior and encourage the pursuit of God's best. Paul instructs Timothy to not be quarrelsome. Then, Paul asks him to be kind to all, able to teach, patient when wronged, and gentle in correction. Talk about five awesome priorities for ministry! May these five traits be true of all leaders in the body of Christ.

6. Sound instruction is emphasized

> *"Now you followed my teaching, conduct, purpose, faith, patience, love, perseverance, persecutions, and sufferings, such as happened to me at Antioch, at Iconium and at Lystra; what persecutions I endured, and out of them all the Lord rescued me!...You, however, continue in the things you have learned and become convinced of, knowing from whom you have learned them, and that from childhood you have known the sacred writings which are able to give you the wisdom that leads to salvation through faith which is in Christ Jesus."* −2 Timothy 3:10-11; 14-15

Hypocrisy is like cancer. It can be around for a long time without being noticed, but in the end, the result is devastating. In this passage, Paul explains the attributes Timothy has learned from him. But he doesn't stop there. Basically, he says "my life lines up with my teaching!" Sound instruction needs to do two things. First, it needs to align with the mentor's own lifestyle. Then, it must permanently alter the recipient. Be the real deal. Teach the real truth. Sound instruction is indispensable.

7. Exhort and encourage

> *"I solemnly charge you in the presence of God and of Christ Jesus, who is to judge the living and the dead, and by His appearing and His kingdom: preach the word; be ready in season and out of season; reprove, rebuke, exhort, with great patience and instruction...But you, be sober in all things, endure hardship, do the work of an evangelist, fulfill your ministry."* −2 Tim. 4:1-2, 5

Birds are fascinating. Think about it. One day, you hatch out of an egg into a nest. Within a few days, you are flying in the air without a pilot's license! If I'm a bird, that first leap out of the nest is either my finest moment or a death sentence. Like a mother bird encourages the little one to fly, mentors speak powerfully into our lives. The labor of love Paul put into Timothy would not have been a good investment if Timothy didn't step out and preach, rebuke, exhort, endure hardship, and fulfill his ministry. Timothy had been prepared for God's calling with intentionality. Now, Paul pushes him out of the nest to learn how to fly.

8. Warn about danger

"Be on guard against him yourself, for he vigorously opposed our teaching" –2 Tim. 4:15

Avoiding danger and difficult people is prudent when launching out in ministry. Good advice from a mentor can save you a world of difficulty. You might see a candle, but your mentor can tell if it's a stick of dynamite! Trusting a mentor who has your best interests in mind may be the lifeline you need.

9. Stay in touch

"Make every effort to come to me soon...The Lord be with your spirit. Grace be with you" –2 Tim. 4:9, 22

God will move people in and out of your life. This can be painful, but it is part of the growth process. God will typically shape you with several mentors over time. These relationships don't have to end, but they will likely change. You don't have to "unfriend" them on Facebook and delete their number on your phone! Even if God moves someone out of your life, it is a wonderful thing to stay in touch and have each other's contact information.

I have spoken with leaders who have a hard time letting mentors go. They feel hurt by the person. They question the value of the relationship and focus on the past. A leadership "refresher" is very helpful in these circumstances.

To maintain balance, you need to keep three types of relationships going at all times: mentoring, being mentored, and having peer relationships. As you lead small groups, God will put you together with many people. You will begin to sense when a mentoring relationship is forming, but also when it is changing. At times, a Christmas card may be your only contact, and that is OK! Keep expectations reasonable. Stay in touch. Be thankful for what God did.

—

Mentoring is the blueprint of legacy. Your influence will rise above teaching and counseling. Counseling involves head-based knowledge, but mentoring involves heart-based knowledge.

Who is your Timothy?

In Christ-centered mentoring, gifts are transferred supernaturally. Your legacy becomes anointed. Efforts have eternal significance Motivation reaches a new level.

May we be forgotten, but God's work remembered!

CHAPTER 13

SALVATION AND BEYOND

Before he ascended into heaven, Jesus told His followers,

"Go therefore and make disciples of all the nations, baptizing them in the name of the Father and the Son and the Holy Spirit, teaching them to observe all that I commanded you."
–Matt. 28:19

Small group leaders have an incredible privilege to make disciples. What must come before discipleship? Salvation. It is the launching point of discipleship. Every follower of Christ should be equipped to minister salvation to others.

Ministering Salvation

Ministering salvation should never be reduced to a formula. Your relationship with the one seeking salvation determines the way you go about it. Ultimately, when there is an opportunity to pray with someone for salvation, invite him or her into relationship with Christ. Have them ask Jesus to be their Lord and Savior. There is no greater joy than knowing God used you to change someone's eternal destination. This joy should motivate us to see people come to Jesus!

Some people want a relationship with Jesus but don't know what they're doing. Salvation can be discussed in great detail, but if nothing else, cover the basics. Explain that sin separates them from God. Jesus paid the penalty for their sin by dying on the cross for them. Have them repent of their sins and ask the Father for forgiveness through Jesus Christ. The resurrection of Jesus Christ conquered their sin and death. This made it possible for them to spend eternity in heaven. The Holy Spirit now lives inside of them (1 Cor. 3:16). He wants to be their spiritual helper (John 16:7).

In the book of Romans, Paul says,

> *"That if you confess with your mouth Jesus as Lord, and believe in your heart that God raised Him from the dead, you will be saved."* –Romans 10:9

There is a connection between the attitude of your heart and the words of your mouth. When leading someone in a prayer for salvation, have him or her *verbally* proclaim Jesus as Lord and Savior. This internalizes the decision. It increases their faith. It fuels belief.

Salvation is a spiritual change, not an emotional one. Some will feel no different. Others may feel completely different! Remind them that their relationship with Christ is based on His promises, not their emotions.

God's not done!

Someone made the decision to have a personal relationship with Jesus! Now what? This is not a one-time event. They've signed up for a lifetime journey with Christ. And, it's wonderful! You can be a source of encouragement and wisdom for them. However, your goal is to create a self-sustaining Christ-follower. To do this, new believers must read God's Word, pray, share their faith, and belong to a Bible-believing church.

New believers don't know where to start when reading the Bible. Tell them to start in John or James. These books are easy to understand and highlight Jesus Christ. Make attainable goals. Tell them to start reading Scripture for 10 minutes a day. Reading God's Word should be their primary spiritual food. Podcasts, Christian books, and their pastor's sermon should not replace their own Bible reading.

Encourage prayer. Pray with them so they can hear an example. They can keep it simple. If they don't know what to pray for, encourage them to start thanking God for a list of His blessings (eg. food to eat, a place to sleep, health). Tell them that they can talk to Jesus like a friend. God loves when they take time to listen to Him.

The more time they spend with God, the more their relationship will grow.

Make them eager to share their experience with others. No Christ-follower is too new to share their faith. Help them develop an effective testimony (Chapter 11).

Get them connected in a Bible-believing church. Every Christian needs to fellowship with other believers (Heb. 10:25). A good church provides corporate worship and opportunities to serve in the body of Christ. These are irreplaceable aspects of discipleship. Don't let a new believer go without it.

Be ready to bring others into relationship with Jesus. In Proverbs it simply says,

"And he who is wise wins souls." –Prov 11:30

Get new believers on the right track with God's Word and prayer. Help them share their faith and plug into a church. If you do this, you'll set them up for a successful journey with Christ.

Destinies will be determined.

Disciples will be made.

His Kingdom will grow!

CHAPTER 14

PRINCIPLES OF PRAYING WITH PEOPLE

Terry had never opened up with anyone. One week at small group, he admitted, "I've crossed the line with my girlfriend. We do things physically that I know aren't right." Terry continued to share about his struggles with pornography and lustful thoughts.

He was trapped in his guilt.

The group of men didn't scold him. They didn't express disappointment.

Instead, they surrounded him with love, laid gentle hands on his shoulders, and prayed. Terry was on the verge of tears.

When the group of men finished praying, Terry looked up in amazement.

"That was the first time I have ever felt the presence of God in my life."

Terry would later become a role model to many men, especially in the area of purity. He grew into one of the most dynamic leaders in our ministry.

Prayer is powerful!

Every small group leader is called to pray with people. Great leaders know when it is time to *play*, and when it is time to *pray*. This can happen at an altar, during small group, or following a one-on-one. Sometimes, prayer is planned ahead. Other times, God opens a door unexpectedly. Understanding these five concepts will offer the confidence needed for effective prayer ministry.

1. Jesus Gave us Spiritual Authority

We have authority to minister in the name of Jesus. That is incredibly powerful! When Jesus sent his disciples out, He *"gave them power and authority over all the demons and to heal diseases"* (Luke 9:1). Likewise, He sends us out with the same power and authority.

God is always good. Sometimes we pray, *"God, if it is your will..."* and continue with the request. All too often, this is evidence of our lack of faith. For example, God always wants to heal. It *is* his will to heal. If I pray, "God, if it is your will to heal this person, please take away the cancer," I set the person up for disappointment. If he or she doesn't experience healing, was it God's will for him or her to have cancer? Certainly not! In Luke 5:12-13, Jesus establishes that physical healing is the will of God. Sometimes, what is in God's *Word* and his *will* is not always in his *wisdom*. Pray with authority over the flesh. Be bold. Bind the work of the enemy in Jesus' name!

2. God is the Power Source

"It's my fault."

Have you ever felt this way after praying intensely for someone? Especially when you see no result?

You are not alone. There is a tendency among Christians to assume too much personal responsibility when praying for people. You hope the eloquence, passion, or length of your prayer boosts the outcome. Bottom line—the results don't depend on us. They depend on God.

Living in Minnesota has given me several opportunities to jump start my car in cold winter months. When I see jumper cables, I am reminded of the attitude I need in prayer. I am the jumper cables. The person receiving prayer is the dead battery, and God is the power source. When I stop praying like it depends on me, God moves in mighty ways.

3. Jesus Gave Examples to Follow

Jesus is the standard of theology. And, since the Bible captures several instances of Jesus praying for people, these examples can be trusted. In Luke 6:18-19, sick people touched Him and they were healed. Many times, Jesus laid hands on the sick (Luke 4:40, Mark 6:5).

Because the laying on of hands is biblical, we highly recommend incorporating this into small group.

Don't be afraid to stop and give a brief explanation. Jesus provided an incredible pattern of prayer. Learn from the best! If it was a good enough for Jesus, it is definitely more than good enough for me!

4. God's character is the basis for prayer

"Dear God, Aunt Cindy is such a kind and loving person. She has done so much for the church, and she has served you faithfully for all these years. We don't know what we would do without her, so please help her find a great job."

While this may be a sincere prayer, it contains a problem. The prayer above appeals to Aunt Cindy's character, not God's character. Although God honors obedience and faithfulness, we can't redeem "good job" points for an answered prayer. When we pray for others, we need to appeal to God's mercy, compassion, love, and justice. God sees past our past. He wants to do the unexpected miracle!

5. Public prayer starts in private

It has been said, "Pray long prayers in private, so you can pray short prayers in public." Jesus set aside substantial time for private prayer (Luke 5:16). And, most would agree that Jesus' public ministry produced rapid results. The best time to pray is before an emergency, not during an emergency.

Pray for your small group on a daily basis. Begin praying now for the group you hope to lead in the future. The hours you spend in private prayer are much more important than the seconds you spend praying in public.

—

Praying for people is an essential component of leading a small group. You will be amazed at what can happen when you ask the simple question, "How can I pray for you?"

Jesus has given you the authority.

Only He can produce the results.

You are the jumper cables God wants to use!

CHAPTER 15

UNDERSTANDING THE BAPTISM IN THE HOLY SPIRIT

Last words are very important. Jesus' were incredibly well-chosen! Before Jesus ascended into heaven, we read,

> *"Gathering them together, He commanded them not to leave Jerusalem, but to wait for what the Father had promised, 'Which,' He said, 'you heard of from Me; for John baptized with water, but you will be baptized with the Holy Spirit not many days from now." –Acts 1:4-5*

Jesus didn't want his followers to hold onto him on earth. He wanted them to embrace the coming Holy Spirit.

Why?

While on earth, Jesus could only be one place at one time. Jesus *"emptied Himself, taking the form of a bond-servant, and being made in the likeness of men"* (Phil 2:7). He limited himself to humanity in order to fully identify with us. After Jesus' death and resurrection, sin was dealt with. The Savior of the world had given his life for our freedom and forgiveness. The grave was defeated. Death was swallowed up in victory (1 Cor. 15:54).

But, God was not done yet! The Holy Spirit was going to open up a new reality for believers—God's presence and power being available anywhere, anytime.

We need the power of the Holy Spirit.

Therefore, we believe in the baptism in the Holy Spirit.

We feel it is imperative for every leader to have a working knowledge of the baptism in the Holy Spirit. To meet this critical need in our ministry, we dedicate two hours of our yearly small group leader retreat to Holy Spirit education. The remainder of this chapter will be a condensed version of that teaching. We will walk through key passages of Scripture pertaining to the Holy Spirit in chronological order.

Every good explanation starts at the beginning. So, let's begin!

The Holy Spirit in the Old Testament

> *"In the beginning God created the heavens and the earth."*
> *—Gen. 1:1*

Let's pause for a quick history lesson. The Old Testament was originally written in Hebrew. In Genesis 1:1, the Hebrew word for "God" is plural, implying the concept of the Trinity. Although the word "Trinity" is not found in Scripture, it is an accurate description of the one true God in three distinct persons: Father, Son (Jesus), and Holy Spirit.

Continuing it says,

> *"The earth was formless and void, and darkness was over the surface of the deep, and the **Spirit** of God was moving over the surface of the waters."—Gen. 1:2 (emphasis added)*

This is Bible's the first reference to the Holy Spirit. The Spirit of God and the Holy Spirit are two names for the same Person, so these terms will be used interchangeably through the remainder of this book. We see that God the Father and the Spirit of God were together, and that the Spirit of God was "moving." The Hebrew word here for "moving" is a continuing action verb that means "to hover and shake." Throughout Genesis 1 and 2, the Holy Spirit is continually moving and hovering throughout the creative process. The spoken word of God combined with the moving of the Holy Spirit brought about the creation of something new.

The same thing happens in our lives today. For example, you might be reading a verse in God's Word about truthfulness. You realize that you struggle with lying and it's a sinful habit. It hurts God and others. You want to change. Stop for a moment! You don't see a flying dove, but the Holy Spirit is hovering and shaking in your life. He wants to perform a creative change inside you. Will you allow him to take away your lying habit and put truth in its place? The Word of God combined with the moving of the Holy Spirit produces change in our lives!

The plurality continues when God creates mankind. He says,

*"Let **Us** make man in **Our** image" – Gen. 1:26,*
(emphasis added)

God's word stamps out the fact that the Father, Son, and Holy Spirit are co-eternal partners in the creative process. There are many other accounts of the Holy Spirit in the Old Testament. For example, Moses, Saul, David and Isaiah all had unique encounters with the Spirit of God (but we won't go into detail in this book). The same Holy Spirit that ignited creation and spoke through the prophets in the Bible is still active today!

The Holy Spirit in the life of Christ

Let's fast forward to Jesus' life. On the last day of the Feast of Tabernacles, Jesus said,

"He who believes in Me, as the Scripture said, from his
innermost being will flow rivers of living water" – John 7:38-39

Here, Jesus reveals a planned event that would empower believers to exude life-giving attributes of the Holy Spirit. Imagine the anticipation this stimulated among Jesus' followers. A promise from Christ can always be trusted!

This might shock you, but the first Easter Sunday had nothing to with eggs or candy! After Jesus rose from the dead, we switched from the Old Covenant to the New Covenant. From being under *law* to being under *grace*. The way God dealt with mankind completely changed. Under the law, punishment for sin was delayed each year through animal sacrifice. This practice could not forgive sin (Heb. 10:4). After Jesus' innocent blood was shed, all sin for all time was forgiven in an instant! Accepting the free gift of forgiveness in Jesus' name became paramount.

Under the Old Covenant, the Holy Spirit could not live inside people. Even when prophets from the Old Testament prophesied, the Holy Spirit would *come upon* them, they would prophesy, and then He would lift. He didn't live inside people...yet! Jesus gave his followers hope with the following words,

> *"Spirit of truth, whom the world cannot receive, because it does not see Him or know Him, but you know Him because He **abides with you and will be in you**." –John 14:16-17, (emphasis added)*

The anticipation continues to increase!

Have you ever had to say goodbye to a close friend who is moving away? If so, you know the mix of emotions. You might feel sad, angry, and even lonely. But, you definitely don't feel happy. How would you like to say goodbye to Jesus?! Talk about the ultimate disappointment!

Easter Sunday came to a close, and the disciples were bummed that their Lord was no longer with them. Wouldn't you be? We are talking about Jesus here!

But, Jesus knows how to make a surprise appearance. Even with the doors locked, Jesus appears and says,

> *"'Peace be with you; as the Father has sent Me, I also send you.' And when He had said this, He breathed on them and said to them, 'Receive the Holy Spirit'" –John 20:21-22*

Now that their salvation had been completed, the Holy Spirit could come and live *inside* of them.

When you accept Jesus as Savior, the Holy Spirit comes to live *inside* of you too. This experience is called salvation. What a beautiful gift!

The Holy Spirit in the Early Church

Shortly before Jesus had ascended into heaven, He gave some important instructions:

> *"Gathering them together, He commanded them not to leave*
> *Jerusalem, but to wait for what the Father had promised,*
> *'Which,' He said, 'you heard of from Me; for John baptized*
> *with water, but you will be baptized with the Holy Spirit not*
> *many days from now'"* —Acts 1:4-5

This promise was quickly approaching!

The coming of the Holy Spirit at salvation (described in the previous section) and the baptism in the Holy Spirit are separate and subsequent experiences. They can happen at virtually the same time. But, in the case of the first disciples, there was a 50-day gap between their salvation and their experience of Spirit baptism.

When I was a freshman in college, I loved Jesus but hadn't been baptized in the Holy Spirit yet. I was the biggest chicken I knew. When I had to walk across campus to small group, I would hide my Bible in my jacket because I was afraid people would tease me. The summer between my freshman and sophomore year of college, I was baptized in the Holy Spirit. I was a completely different person when I showed up on campus in the fall. The chicken in me left, and a boldness flowed through me. I began intentionally inviting people to small group and church, and they came with me! Praise God for this extraordinary experience!

God loves to be consistent. In Acts, there are four recorded instances of the baptism in the Holy Spirit. Some include a fifth instance where Paul is baptized in the Holy Spirit (Acts 9). Although they are each unique, one common thread is evident: speaking in tongues. This is either directly stated or strongly inferred. Let's walk through each instance briefly.

Acts 2 - Jewish Christians wait at Pentecost

> *"When the day of Pentecost had come, they were all together in*
> *one place. And suddenly there came from heaven a noise like*
> *a violent rushing wind, and it filled the whole house where*
> *they were sitting. And there appeared to them tongues as of fire*
> *distributing themselves, and they rested on each one of them.*
> *And they were all filled with the Holy Spirit and began to speak*
> *with other tongues, as the Spirit was giving them utterance."*
> —Acts 2:1-4

Pentecost remains a significant feast in Jewish culture. It marks the beginning of the barley harvest. God did not pour out His Spirit during this festival by accident. In this moment, God would empower His people to bring in an anticipated harvest not of wheat, but of souls into His Kingdom!

Two phenomena in this passage are never documented in Scripture again: a wind sound and fire. Why don't these phenomena happen in later instances? It comes down to the lack of previous experience. God does not try to be confusing! All 120 believers at the scene were Jewish Christians. Jesus had told them to wait in the Jerusalem and experience something that nobody else in history had ever experienced. How would the disciples know when it was happening? God showed them in a way they could understand. Three primary symbols signified the Holy Spirit in the Old Testament: wind, fire, and oil. So, the wind sound and fire would have immediately tipped them off—this was the Spirit baptism that Jesus had been talking about! They also began to speak in tongues as the Spirit enabled them!

Acts 8 - Simon and the Samaritans

"Then they began laying their hands on them, and they were receiving the Holy Spirit. Now when Simon saw that the Spirit was bestowed through the laying on of the apostles' hands, he offered them money." —Acts 8:17-18

In this instance, the people who received the Baptism in the Holy Spirit weren't fully Jewish. They were Samaritans, which means they were descendants of Israelites who intermarried with the pagan nations within Canaan. This demonstrates that God was not playing favorites (with this gift) based on heritage. The gift was indeed, *"for you and your children and for all who are far off, as many as the Lord our God will call to Himself"* (Acts 2:39).

Although the words "speaking in tongues" are not specifically stated, this event occurred within five years of the original Pentecost experience. We have good reason to believe this instance was similar to Pentecost, since the text doesn't tell us otherwise. Although the passage doesn't describe it, whatever Simon (a sorcerer) saw, he could tell it was the Holy Spirit being imparted and was impressed by it. He even offered the apostles money for their abilities! Obviously, this was a bad request for two reasons. First, Simon was looking only to benefit himself. Second, the baptism in the Holy Spirit is a *gift*! It can't be bought—Jesus gives it freely!

Acts 10: Cornelius' household

"All the circumcised believers who came with Peter were amazed, because the gift of the Holy Spirit had been poured out on the Gentiles also. For they were hearing them speaking with tongues and exalting God." –Acts 10:45-46

Cornelius was Italian—there wasn't a drop of Jewish blood in him! We have to understand that in this time, Jews had an intense racial and religious prejudice against non-Jews (or Gentiles). They wouldn't even eat with them. Peter was breaking the cultural barrier just being in Cornelius' house. Now, Cornelius' entire household was experiencing salvation and the baptism in the Holy Spirit with the evidence of speaking in tongues! Peter and other Jewish Christians were observing in amazement. The moving of the Holy Spirit was accelerating at a rapid rate!

Acts 19 - Ephesian believers

"And when Paul had laid his hands upon them, the Holy Spirit came on them, and they began speaking with tongues and prophesying." –Acts 19:6

Twenty years later, it is still happening! These believers loved Jesus, but the Scripture tells us they didn't have much information about the Holy Spirit. They hadn't even heard of the Holy Spirit! Paul prayed for these Ephesians and they began speaking in tongues and prophesying. The pattern is evident—when people receive the baptism of the Holy Spirit, they speak in tongues.

—

One key message must be stressed: these instances involve the personal use of praying in tongues to God. The evidence of speaking in tongues in prayer, after being baptized in the Holy Spirit, is available to all Christ followers. This experience is distinct from the Spiritual gift of tongues, where the audience is other people, and it requires interpretation (1 Cor. 14:27). When I pray in English, my mind tells my mouth what to say. When I pray in tongues, the Holy Spirit tells my mouth what to pray.

Praying in tongues is an incredibly valuable tool. Paul summarizes this beautifully, by saying,

> *"In the same way the Spirit also helps our weakness; for we do not know how to pray as we should, but the Spirit Himself intercedes for us with groanings too deep for words."*
> *—Rom. 8:26*

Paul later says,

> *"I speak in tongues more than you all"* *—1 Cor. 14:18*

Most of us agree that we don't really know how to say the right prayer. In my life, instances happen every day where prayers from my intellect are terribly inadequate. The Spirit knows exactly what's going on. He is all-knowing! You can pray in line with God's will by praying what you know (in your own language) and then taking time to pray in tongues (your spiritual prayer language). You might also hear the phrase "praying in the Spirit," which is used interchangeably with "praying in tongues" in Scripture (1 Cor. 14:14). This is effective because we don't always know the details, but the Holy Spirit knows all the details!

Praying in tongues to God is not a one-time event. It is a wonderful lifestyle of unbiased prayer and increasing passion for those who don't know Christ. It is available to those who ask (Luke 11:13) and builds our faith (Jude 20). We encourage leaders to pursue the Baptism in the Holy Spirit and pray in the Spirit on a daily basis. *Appendix 1* contains helpful directions on how to pray with someone to receive the baptism in the Holy Spirit one-on-one.

The baptism in the Holy Spirit is not a badge of honor. It is not a requirement for salvation. However, praying in tongues is a powerful tool that empowers us to reach our workplaces, campuses, and families more effectively for Christ.

Jesus declares,

> *"...but you will receive power when the Holy Spirit has come upon you; and you shall be My witnesses both in Jerusalem, and in all Judea and Samaria, and even to the remotest part of the earth"* *—Acts 1:8*

This message is for you and me.

Jerusalem is your city.

Judea and Samaria is your region.

Let's reach the world in Jesus' name with the power of the Holy Spirit.

CHAPTER 16

THE PRACTICAL USE OF SPIRITUAL GIFTS

Jesus asked his disciples to wait for the Holy Spirit. It was worth the wait! It changed the church forever. The same Holy Spirit is active today and plays a critical role in reaching our world. Why would I ever choose to lead a small group, or any form of ministry, without His power? The Holy Spirit should be key player in whatever we are doing.

There are new ministry tactics being developed every day (eg. new books, conferences, and outreach ideas). But, do they tap into the Holy Spirit's power? It is imperative we use the power of the Holy Spirit in our everyday ministry. Our goal should be to teach others to do the same.

Unfortunately, many stay away from the gifts of the Holy Spirit (or Spiritual gifts, terms used interchangeably) for one of the following reasons: a negative experience, a lack of confidence, or simple ignorance. So, why emphasize Spiritual gifts? Why are they important? They empower people to effectively advance the Kingdom of God. The Holy Spirit helps people overcome sin, share Christ, and operate in Spiritual gifts.

Jen came to church to give God one last chance. God was ready. At the end of the message, a gentleman came to the front and shared a word of knowledge with the group and said, "Someone here has a deep hurt that occurred at the age of 16, and you are unable to forgive God. But God wants you to know He loves you." Jen knew that he was talking about her because she carried a hurt that occurred on her 16th birthday! The presence of God immediately touched her. At that moment, she knew God cared for her, and she needed to make Jesus Christ the Lord of her life. Jen is going to heaven because one person was willing to be obedient to the Holy Spirit.

Souls hang in the balance every day. Someone in your life may be ready to make a commitment to Christ. What if God wants to make that move through a Spiritual gift? Jesus Christ promised this power to us. Make the decision to reach out and grab it. The following five steps will help you get ready to be used in a Spiritual gift.

Understand the Source of the Power

Spiritual gifts are fueled by the baptism in the Holy Spirit. For a refresher on what the Bible says about this incredible experience and how to pray with someone to receive it, refer back to Chapter 15 and *Appendix 1*. The baptism in the Holy Spirit is the spark plug that ignites the gifts. He allows them to flow from you in a greater way.

Understand What the Gifts Are

Some become confused when trying to define a gift of the Holy Spirit. You don't have to be stumped. The Bible clearly outlines these gifts:

> *"For to one is given the **word of wisdom** through the Spirit, and to another the **word of knowledge** according to the same Spirit; to another **faith** by the same Spirit, and to another **gifts of healing** by the one Spirit, and to another the **effecting of miracles**, and to another **prophecy**, and to another the **distinguishing of spirits**, to another **various kinds of tongues**, and to another the **interpretation of tongues.**"*
> *—1 Cor. 12:8-10 (emphasis added)*

In this book, I won't go into depth about each of these Spiritual gifts. However, know that each of them can be administered to any believer at any time (1 Cor. 12:7). In brief, a Spiritual gift is God giving you the ability to know, say, or do something that you would never have been able to formulate in your own power. You are used in a way that is above human ability or knowledge.

Understand Heart Alignment

Spiritual gifts are all about God's glory. They are meant to give glory to God and show it to others. It has nothing to do with you. Your part is simply obeying. If you seek to be used in a Spiritual gift just so you have a cool story, God will not move. You must align your heart with God's heart. Instead of praying to be used in a Spiritual gift, pray that your heart would align with God's heart. Pray that He would use you in whatever way He asks. This prayer is powerful because it takes away any self-seeking motivations.

Habitual sin in your life makes it difficult to clearly hear from the Holy Spirit. Ephesians 4:29-32 explains that actions have the ability to grieve the Holy Spirit, leading to inactivity. However, this does not mean you need to be perfect to be used in this way. If that were the case, no one would ever flow in a Spiritual gift. God's grace is powerful, but you must make sure that your heart is right before God. This ensures He has full access to flow through you.

Understand How to Hear

God speaks to people in different ways. There is no set formula for hearing the Holy Spirit's voice. I believe many people reading this book have been used in a Spiritual gift already but didn't realize it. This is simply due to a misunderstanding or lack of knowledge. I'll describe some typical ways you can hear the voice of the Holy Spirit.

The Holy Spirit can speak through spontaneous thoughts. In other words, you *think* it. All of a sudden, you're thinking about someone you haven't thought of in a while. The Holy Spirit may be prompting you to action. Start praying for that person. Give them a call. Tell them you love them and pray together if you have the opportunity. You may be surprised at the response you receive.

You *might* see it. While praying for someone, God might show you a picture in your mind. It may be of someone or something. Pray for wisdom and ask God what it means. Ask if it should be shared with a particular person. Even if it doesn't make sense to you, it likely makes complete sense to the person needing the message.

You can *feel* it. When Jesus was walking through the crowd and was touched by the woman with the issue of bleeding, he felt power leave him (Mark 5:25-34). I believe the Holy Spirit can speak to us through physical and emotional feelings. If you ask God to use you,

He may speak to you in unusual ways. If your right knee starts to hurt, and there is no reason for it to be hurting, that might be the Holy Spirit speaking to you. Maybe He desires to heal someone's knee! The Holy Spirit speaks to many leaders in our ministry through this method. It leads to subsequent words of knowledge, and healings occur.

You may feel emotionally attacked for no reason. Pray and ask God for wisdom. I've seen these feelings prompt a word of knowledge, which led to someone being healed of depression. The Holy Spirit's work is truly amazing.

Don't overcomplicate this. The Holy Spirit does not intend his business to be difficult. The more you respond to His promptings, the easier it will become to discern His voice.

You think God gave you a word of knowledge that He wants to heal someone's broken wrist. You share it with the group, but no one responds! Were you wrong? Not necessarily. Don't be discouraged. The person may have felt uncomfortable or scared. Even if you were wrong, God knows you're trustworthy! I've found that I'm OK being wrong a few times to see the Holy Spirit work multiple times!

When God gives you a message to share, you might be tempted to doubt it. Instead of asking, "what if I am wrong?" ask yourself, "what if I am right?" God will use this boldness to change lives.

Understand Communication

This point is arguably the most important of all. If you can't properly communicate what the Lord spoke, it has the potential to cause more harm than good. A rifle is safe and effective when handled correctly and aimed in the right direction. God's power is entrusted to you in a similar way.

> *"For some men, straying from these things, have turned aside to fruitless discussion, wanting to be teachers of the Law, even though they do not understand either what they are saying or the matters about which they make confident assertions."*
> *—2 Tim. 1:6-7*

You cannot neglect the words "love" and "self-discipline" in this passage. God's power must be communicated with love. The power of

God and the love of God always work together. God did not intend for Spiritual gifts to be mystical or theatrical. God is practical. His gifts can be communicated in a practical ways to meet practical needs.

When we feel that the Holy Spirit prompting us to operate in a gift, we need to start praying. What does He want to say or do? Are there more details he wants to tell us? Discern whether He wants to speak to the group or an individual. The Holy Spirit usually has a specific time, place, and target audience for a spiritual gift. He may tell you to share right away. It might be a blessing for someone later. Trust his direction.

Explain to others what's happening when the Holy Spirit moves. It may be the first time someone has seen a gift of the Holy Spirit displayed. Help them understand by showing them examples in Scripture. Express God's love.

Spiritual gifts will always reflect the heart of God. They should never produce emotional destruction. The Holy Spirit will bring conviction (John 16:8), but never condemnation, shame, or guilt.

Believe you can be used in spiritual gifts. One of my favorite stories in the Bible is when the man gets healed at Gate Beautiful in Acts 3. Peter follows up this miracle by asking two very interesting questions:

> "But when Peter saw this, he replied to the people, 'Men of Israel, why are you amazed at this, or why do you gaze at us, as if by our own power or piety we had made him walk?'"
> —Acts 3:12

These questions tell us two very important things about the supernatural power of God. First, it should be common and expected in our ministries. The same God that raised Christ from the dead lives in every one of us (Rom. 8:11)! We should minister to people with the expectation that his power will show up!

Second, it doesn't require special qualifications to access. A common misconception is that Spiritual gifts are only for evangelists, pastors, and other prominent spiritual leaders. However, Peter tells us that it's not about being in a high position. It's about one's obedience and willingness to be used by God. And when you are obedient, you'll inspire others to be used by the Holy Spirit too!

Brian was depressed and alone when he came to our weekly worship service. He had served God as a young man, but was really beginning to doubt his relationship with God. He came to our meeting with the intention of giving God one last try. Before he entered, he prayed a simple prayer, *"God, if you are real, show me that you love me, and that I belong in this ministry."* During the meeting, a complete stranger sitting next to Brian leaned over, put his arm around him, and said, *"God wants me to tell you that He loves you, and that you belong here."* Brian's life was changed forever.

The Holy Spirit is powerful.

His gifts are practical.

Don't do ministry without Him.

CHAPTER 17

Developing a Small Group Ministry Structure

A lot of training material has been covered in this book. We realize that every small group ministry has unique needs and goals. Ministries may refer to their smaller communities as "small groups", "life groups", "core groups", or another similar term. Even this demonstrates that there is no one "right way" to navigate this topic.

If your structure works, we aren't telling you to change it. We understand that some of the things we do may work great for us but not for others. However, some of you may be interested in the specifics of our small group ministry. In this chapter, I'll share with you the strategies we've developed to make our small groups succeed—with an enormous amount of God's help!

Effective Leadership Training

One of the keys to successful small group ministry is effective leadership training. Every year in late March, we have a small group leader retreat. We invite all new and existing leaders to attend. New leaders appreciate having their mentors (existing leaders) present, and mentors enjoy seeing their spiritual sons and daughters (new leaders) formalize their leadership role. We primarily rely on our existing leaders to identify individuals who would be great small group leaders the following year.

The retreat consists of 10 hours of teaching on a Friday night and Saturday morning. It usually takes place at our church (in town) so that traveling and cost aren't barriers for attendance. For the retreat, each person is given a manual to follow along with that coincides with the content of this book. Friday night includes a time of everyone getting into smaller groups, telling each other what they love about each other. Saturday morning concludes with an opportunity to officially sign-up to become small group leader in the next small group cycle.

Ongoing Leadership Development

Leaders must be given opportunities to continually grow. Without ongoing leadership development, a leader's potential is squandered. One of my hobbies is working in my garden. If the only time I watered and took care of it was the day I planted it, I would be setting myself up for disappointment. Likewise, neglecting ongoing leadership development limits people from being all that God desires them to be.

To encourage and develop leaders during the year, we utilize multiple tactics. The first is to provide every leader with a mentoring one-on-one each month. In order to make this possible, we have developed a team solely dedicated to discipling small group leaders. This incredible team is called the "Fan Team." Each Fan Team member accepts 2-15 small group leaders to mentor. The group consists of ministry interns and former small group leaders who live in the area. We couldn't accomplish this great task of ongoing discipleship without them!

We also have a monthly meeting for all small group leaders called "Converge." It is a time to discuss deeper leadership topics, communicate vision, and go over the details of special events. There are light refreshments, including muffins and coffee. We consistently encourage our leaders to be outwardly focused at our large group meetings, so Converge is a valued time to just be together. In the early fall, we have a one-day "mini-retreat" before a new season of small groups begin. This event helps everyone regroup and rejuvenate vision.

Leadership Requirements

One very common question among pastors overseeing small group ministries is, "what are your requirements for leaders?" The Bible says to *"abstain from every form of evil." –1 Thess. 5:22*

We never want our liberties to cause others to stumble. Therefore, we ask leaders to uphold three to five guidelines to help them live above reproach. It is always better to pursue God's best. What values and qualities are non-negotiable for you and your ministry? As a pastor, it is important to make these expectations clear and give sound reasoning of why the standards are so important. In turn, small group leaders are blessed when they honor the authority of their pastor.

Recommended Reading

We are often asked what Christian reading materials we recommend to leaders. In today's world, there is an endless amount of great Christian books. All the resources make it difficult to recommend great books for leaders to read. For the last six years, we have recommended that all leaders read the following three books as they are able:

1. *The Holy Spirit and You* - Dennis and Rita Bennett

2. *Why Revival Tarries* - Leonard Ravenhill

3. *Undercover* - John Bevere

These three books go in-depth on the Holy Spirit, prayer, and spiritual authority, respectively. We have been told countless times by leaders that these are "must-reads." Currently, these books are available online and are relatively inexpensive, especially if they are used books.

—

You may be ready to make a change in the way you do small group ministry. Sometimes, the biggest hurdle is simply putting handles on the next step. Strategically developing a structure can be difficult. Often times, small adjustments are the best. When in doubt, seek input from others who lead good small groups.

No model or strategy can replace the anointing that is needed to reach people for Christ. If you lead a small group ministry, your leaders are craving your wisdom. Share your heart at every opportunity. Leaders will be quick to share your love for people and for Jesus Christ.

CONCLUSION

The two passages of Scripture I want engraved on my tombstone are 1 Thessalonians 2:7-8 and Ephesians 4:29. I featured the passage from 1 Thessalonians in my introduction, so I think it is fitting to discuss Ephesians 4:29 here. The verse says,

> *"Let no unwholesome word proceed from your mouth, but only such a word as is good for edification according to the need of the moment, so that it will give grace to those who hear."*
> *–Eph. 4:29*

Everyone who aspires to be a person of influence needs to have a revelation of how powerful their words are. Ephesians 4:29 offers two powerful instructions and an incredible promise.

The first instruction is, *"Let no unwholesome word come out of your mouth."* As a small group leader, there is never a good reason to use negative or degrading words. There is a way to be honest without cutting someone down. Remember,

> *"The mouth of the righteous is the fountain of life..."*
> *–Prov 10:11*

The second command is to, *"edify according to the need of the moment."* All people have needs, but they may not always be ready for your edifying word. You still need to share it! The Holy Spirit will use it at the proper time to extend grace or wisdom. What a promise! If we are faithful to share an edifying word, the Holy Spirit will bring a harvest.

Several years ago, one of my interns was struggling with his self-worth. I told him, *"I believe in you."* These four words changed his life. Be ready for your words to have great influence in peoples' lives.

As I have shared the things God has taught me in this book, I pray it will be the word of edification you need in this moment. In Christ, you have what it takes to be a person of influence. I am excited about the lives that are going to change through your obedience to the great God that we serve! All glory to Jesus Christ!

RESOURCES AND WEBSITES

FM Chi Alpha: www.fmchialpha.com

Twitter: @fmchialpha

XALeader Small Group Resource Blog: www.xaleader.com

Twitter: @xaleader

APPENDIX 1

Principles for Ministering the Baptism in the Holy Spirit One-on-One

1. Comfortable and private setting.

2. Make sure they are born again.

3. Cover these Scriptures:

   • Luke 11:9-13 – Have to ask and will receive

   • John 7:37-39 – Comes from innermost being

   • Acts 2:1-4 – They spoke

   • Acts 19:1-16 – 20 years after Pentecost still happening

4. Give them the opportunity to deal with unforgiveness or unconfessed sin.

5. Tell them what will happen. Create an atmosphere for faith.

6. Lead them in a prayer, asking Jesus to baptize them in the Holy Spirit with the evidence of speaking in other tongues and thanking God in advance for what He is going to do.

7. Lay hands on them and say, "Receive the Holy Spirit." Then begin to quietly pray in tongues yourself.

8. After they start speaking in tongues, have them start and stop a couple of times.

9. Deal with the devil's lies. (e.g. "You're making this up")

P.S. If they are skeptical or not ready, send them home with a book, such as *Holy Spirit and You*. Wait to pray for them.

ABOUT THE AUTHOR

Pastor Brad Lewis, BS, MS, has been a college ministry director for 26 years, overseeing a multi-staff, multi-site movement on the campuses of North Dakota State University and Minnesota State University – Moorhead. Brad currently pastors over 700 college students and over 140 small group leaders who attend one of four weekly services. In his first book, *Small Group University*, Brad reveals practical steps for effective discipleship and keys to heartfelt small group community. Brad earned a Bachelor's and Master's degree from North Dakota State University and frequently ministers alongside his wife of 20 years, Kay. Brad Lewis is a highly sought after ministry coach, mentor, and nationally recognized thought leader within Chi Alpha, the college ministry arm of the Assemblies of God. He also serves as the College Pastor at First Assembly Church in Fargo, ND.

Made in the USA
Columbia, SC
22 July 2022

63828998R00067